Babs Behan

by hand

Botanical
Dyes

Plant-to-Print Dyes, Techniques and Projects

Photography by Kim Lightbody

Hardie Grant

QUADRILLE

contents

1 botanical dyes

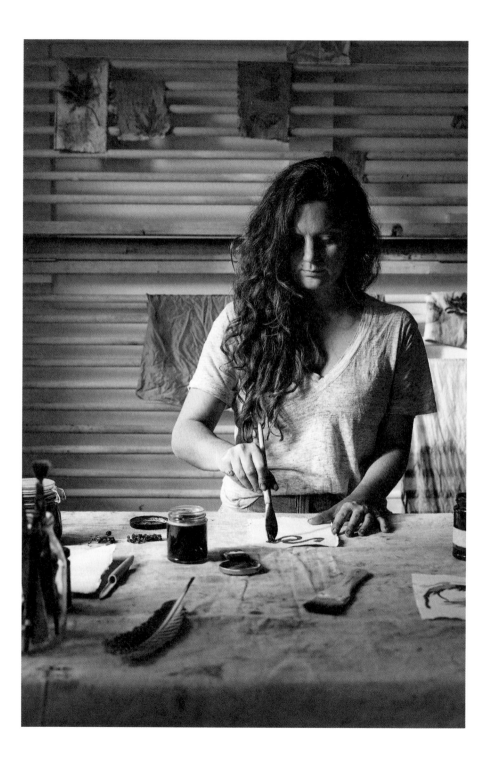

the author

I first became aware of natural dyeing and printing processes when a friend told me about a vegetable dye block-printing factory in India. I had studied BA Surface Design at the University of the Arts London, but was concerned about all the synthetic chemicals that were used, which got on my skin and diffused into the air. When I arrived at the studio each day I was hit by a wall of toxic vapour and it didn't feel safe to be working in this way for long periods of time. I wanted to find a more sustainable and natural way forward, so I arranged an internship in Jaipur, India, at the factory my friend had visited. It turned out to be a fascinating and life-changing experience.

Murghal-style block printing has an elegant look: hand-carved teak blocks and vegetable inks create delicate prints on cloth and Khadi paper. It's a practice that has been handed down through generations, but is now mostly a vanishing tradition due to the increasing demand for synthetic screen- and roll-printing. I fell in love with the quality of line the wooden blocks produced, the earthy colours of the syrupy plant dyes, the skill of the artisans and the sophistication of their handcrafted work.

I learned how to carve wooden blocks based on my own illustrations, to play with repeat patterns and to use vegetable inks on cotton and silk. I also discovered the vintage silk sari recycling industry, which seemed a more sustainable way to produce clothing – using cloth that already existed and had a second life left in it, rather than creating more. This led me to create a clothing line that focused on using natural fibres and recycling vintage cloth into colourful, expressive, bohemian garments, which I sold through independent boutiques in the UK.

Meanwhile, I travelled to explore other cultures and different ways of living and seeing the world – and I was fascinated to find that dyeing using plant materials is still thriving in many areas. Everywhere I went, I learned what I could about the natural dyes specific to each place. In Laos, I made dyes using madder and indigo, and dyed skeins of peace silk with traditional textile institution Ock Pop Tok to make the most lustrous shades of blood red

and midnight blue. In the Sacred Valley of Peru, I stayed for a week with a Quechuan master dyer in his family home at 2,000 metres altitude, where we brewed large cauldrons of plant material into vibrant shades of bright pink, soft turquoise, deep green, scarlet red and mustard yellow. In Indonesia, I explored batik painting with wax on bolts of cotton. In southern India, I learned about the local natural dyeing and weaving industry.

After six years of the travelling artisan lifestyle, I was ready for a change. International supply chains no longer made any sense to me – instead I dreamed of the re-emergence of a local manufacturing system that used locally sourced fibre and natural plant dyes. I spent the summer of 2013 on an artist residency in the Cotswolds, developing a palette of dyes made from local hedgerow plants. I loved the magic of creating colour from the plants around me, infused with their unique herbal essences. I created clothing that spoke of the land, and my wardrobe became filled with meaningful garments that gave me a sense of place and felt restorative and empowering, like herbal charms. I began to teach what I had learned to others, sharing the pleasure of foraging plants for colour and connecting with nature in a new and interesting way.

This led me to found Botanical Inks, an artisan natural dye studio based in Bristol, England (see overleaf). Ultimately, I hope that this work will encourage cultural change in the way we create things. That we will re-adopt some of the old tried-and-tested processes, and combine them with our contemporary skills and technology, so that we can work in a way that is more responsible for people and the planet.

botanical inks

There is so much joy that comes from colour and nature. My studio, Botanical Inks, was founded in order to explore what's available in the natural world, and to reduce the impact of the textile and creative industries on the environment and people.

Botanical Inks first began by offering workshops in the natural dye techniques I had learned and developed from my travels, with an emphasis on using materials and tools that are of the earth, safe to work with and can be put back into the ground at the end of their useful life cycle without risk. I like to work with local farmers, growers, weavers and mills to source and use 100% organic, natural dyes, mordants, cloth and paper. I also use natural fibre tools, such as wooden printing blocks, brushes and string. The people who attend the workshops seem to respond to these holistic, authentic practices and this way of extracting colours from plants. They feel inspired by making natural dyes, paints, drawing and printing inks, and using them in textile and paper surface design techniques.

Understanding the natural colour palette of a particular bio-region, and creating art with materials that you have made with your own hands and from the plants that grow around you, can be an incredibly enriching, empowering and connective experience. There is something simple and beautiful about walking out onto the land and picking up fallen leaves, harvesting flowers and berries, and digging up muddy roots, and then soaking them in water to extract their colour.

I have seen people falling in love over and over again with these old-new ways of creating something – they love the fact that bringing more beauty into the world needn't be harmful to the environment or to their personal health. I have a drive to share these skills, because they are otherwise not easily found. I want to make it easier for others to use natural materials for their creative pursuits, and for those in industry to see that they are commercially viable for their work, too.

Following the popularity of the workshops, Botanical Inks started creating limited-edition handmade naturally dyed products and bespoke services. These include bundle-dyed silk scarves; a bridal bouquet recycling service to make silk lingerie and keepsakes; waste food-dyed table linens; wild writing inks; and block-printed gift cards. These not only add something radical to the marketplace and challenge the status quo, but also demonstrate the high level of sustainable practice that is possible in the UK.

It feels important to create a local system like this, not only for the environment, but also for society. It's amazing to be able to invest in something made within the community, using local resources and traditional skills that are characteristic of the culture. It strengthens our sense of community, as well as our relationship with the local land and nature.

For people at home starting out on a small scale, this last point about connecting with nature is perhaps key. Modern life involves more time spent indoors, and fewer opportunities to interact with plants, animals and wild landscapes. Spending time outdoors – and developing playful relationships with natural materials – allows us to reconnect with our environment and cultivate an affinity for the natural world. Botanical Inks has allowed me to do this, and I hope this book helps you to do the same.

how to use this book

This book has been written as a guide and companion for the home dyer – natural dyeing isn't an exact science, and there is no one right way to do it. It's best to travel through the book from front to back, as the first two chapters, Fibres, Mordants and Modifiers, and Making Dyes, provide you with all the basic information you need to get started. Much of the book refers back to these chapters, which cover how to prepare your fabrics, as well as how to make and use dye baths. The Dye Colours chapter goes on to list some of the most popular dye materials you can find or buy, and gives an overview of their characteristics, as well as tips on how to prepare and use them. The Dyeing Techniques chapter explores applying natural colour and print to textiles. And lastly, the Projects chapter offers a selection of ideas to help you turn your dyed textiles into wonderful gifts and items – use these as inspiration for your own creative journey.

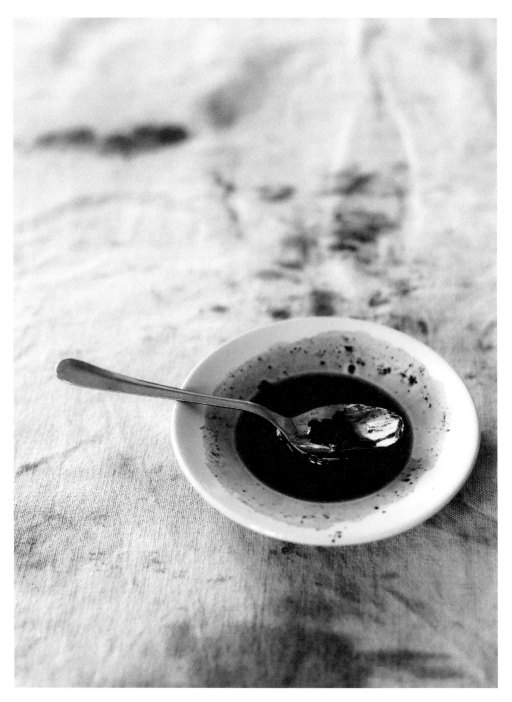

natural dyeing

Natural dyes are extracted from natural sources, such as plants, fungi, minerals and insects. Plants provide the largest range of natural colours, from leaves, flowers and roots, to berries, nuts, seeds, wood and bark. Mineral dyes use pigments from earth and rocks, such as ochre and umber. Insect dyes are made from cochineal, kermes and lac insects. These sources, being naturally of the earth, are often full of vitamins, minerals and herbal qualities.

Natural dyes can be used with textiles – 'in the fleece', the yarn, the cloth or the finished sewn piece. They can also be applied directly onto paper surfaces and other natural materials, such as shells, leather, wood and ceramics. The colour achieved has lustre and depth because it is made up of many particles of varying colour – unlike a synthetic dye colour, which is composed of only one or two single pigments and appears flat. Also, because natural dyes contain so many colour particles, different dye colours complement each other rather than jar as synthetic dyes sometimes do. It feels warming to the soul to know and feel that the materials you use to create beautiful things are in themselves full of beauty, safe to use and might even nourish the skin, body and wider environment.

history of natural dyeing
Deriving colour from natural resources is believed to have developed simultaneously around the world during the Neolithic period, which began around 10,000 BC. Evidence from this period shows that natural pigments from minerals were used to paint cave walls, shells, stones, hides and feathers. However, paints sit on the surface, so are different from dyes, which bond with the fibre. It is difficult to trace the historical use of natural dyes because of the lack of written records and the nature of dyed materials, which erode and decay quickly unless they are very well preserved.

The earliest written records of dyeing date back to China in 2600 BC, with recipes for red, black and yellow dyes. Examples of natural-dyed textiles have been found preserved in the tomb of Tutankhamun and in pre-Incan burial tombs. There are references to scarlet linen in the Bible, and to dyed robes in the writings of Alexander the Great and the great writers Dioscorides, Pliny the Elder and Herodotus. In the Middle Ages, those with plant knowledge – healers, herbalists, midwives and natural dyers – are believed to have steeped their undergarments in their brews and tonics to wear against the most sensitive parts of their skin and absorb their healing properties. Unfortunately many of these wise people were denounced as witches and executed, but a few went into hiding and continued to pass their skills onto later generations, keeping the plant knowledge alive until it could safely be practised again.

Across the globe through history, natural dyes and fibres have been characterised by local bio-regions: the natural resources available in a particular place that help shape the potential for colour, the ways in which fibre is manipulated, and the tools and methods with which the colour is applied. Some places are fortunate to have plants that provide exciting colours, such as the bright pinks and red of sappanwood in India, the deep rare blues of indigo from the tropics, the vivid pinks of cochineal from Mexico, and the revered Tyrian purple of the ancient Phoenicians from the west Mediterranean.

Some dyes were so rare and valuable that they were reserved solely for royalty as status symbols. Tyrian purple, for example, was worth its weight in gold as a result of its laborious production, which involved crushing thousands of sea snails to capture their purple secretions. As a result its brilliant purple only adorned the cloaks of kings and priests.

In Europe, the range of colours tended towards softer hues: gentle pinks, yellows, earthy oranges and browns, and light greens. They are delicate and beautiful in their own right, sitting well with the soft landscape and natural colours of the flora and fauna.

The development of colour palettes was also connected to the discovery of new mordants to help fix colours. Alum and iron were used as mordants in ancient Egypt and India, while medieval dyers are believed to have used iron, copper, alum and tin. In places where access to such metals was limited, plant-based mordants such as rhubarb, club moss and oak gall were used. Other possibilities were seawater, soymilk, staghorn sumac, juniper needles, symplocos, stale urine and naturally iron-rich mud.

As more trade routes opened up, with tropical dye materials travelling back from China and the Americas, the use of brighter dyes became popular with the wealthiest European families. Dye materials were often considered the perfect shipping commodity: they were rare, high value, low in volume, and long lasting enough to survive extended journeys. By the 18th century, British colonialism saw the development of large-scale operations to meet the demands of a growing consumer culture, while the Industrial Revolution in Europe led to mass production.

But as machines replaced people in textile and paper factories, standards for dye colour and colourfastness became more demanding. Chemists began to find ways of extracting isolated colour particles from dyes to make more intensely saturated colours and eventually discovered techniques for taking colour from the by-products of the coal industry. In the mid-19th century, William Perkin was the first to develop a coal-tar-derived dye, mauvine, while trying to find a form of synthetic quinine as a cure for malaria. An explosion in the availability of different chemical dyes followed, which completely overtook the use of natural dyes.

Still, more traditional ways of working did survive. The Arts and Crafts movement that flourished in Britain and spread to Europe and America from 1880 to 1920 stood for the preservation of traditional craftsmanship in the fine and decorative arts. Its members were against the advancements of industry, advocating simple form, natural materials, quality and the journey of the making process itself. William Morris was one of the movement's pioneers, and he had a preference for the pure shades offered by plants in his work, which was inspired by spending time in nature. Morris created beautifully intricate printed wallpapers and textiles, using natural dyes such as indigo, walnut, cochineal, kermes and madder. He was also deeply concerned about the wellbeing of his workers and industrial pollution. In the late 19th century his factories were some of the few to use traditional and more ecological techniques for dyeing and printing.

current context
Today, the use of natural dyes is mainly limited to home and craft dyers, traditional artisans and a handful of commercial-scale units around the world. But the detrimental environmental impact of synthetic chemicals is becoming more commonly acknowledged. The health of workers in synthetic dye industries is often compromised, with skin diseases, respiratory problems and other health issues and even fatalities reportedly associated. But it's not only those involved in the supply chains of these materials who are at risk – consumers who wear or handle items containing certain synthetic chemicals could also be absorbing toxins into their skin.

The extensive use of water in synthetic dye manufacturing processes is problematic in itself, but more concerning is how contaminated that water becomes. Waste water from the textile dyeing industry is notorious as one of the most polluting in the world. Can we afford to wait for governing bodies to clamp down on the social and environmental impact of these industries, and for the corporations responsible to become accountable for their effect on people and the planet?

By being more aware of how things are made and reach us, we can start to think about what we want to support. We need more solutions and better alternatives for people to invest in, which means more independent designers and makers, using local, organic, responsibly sourced materials and low-impact production, with an awareness of environmental and social impact at the heart of their work. A change in consumer demand would perhaps be the most effective solution for ending the damaging way things are made. Then we could start to move away from synthetic dyes, textiles, paints, inks and drawing materials. In fact, it's encouraging to see a resurgence of interest in slower lifestyles and more ecological approaches to design.

Natural dyes cost the earth far less and can also be cheaper to produce than chemical-based mass-market options. Most popular dye plants can be grown easily in a garden, allotment or community growing space. There is great charm and beauty in using, wearing and surrounding yourself in the colours of your own environment – it's an invitation to feel more connected to the land.

botanical dyes

sourcing dye material

There are endless sources of natural dye colours around us, from the domestic (household and garden) to the public (local parks, woodlands and wildernesses). Once you start developing your eco-literacy for natural colour, you will start to see colour potential everywhere you look.

Whatever dye material you find or choose – whether it's freshly foraged plants or dried dye material from specialist suppliers – this book will guide you in turning it into a dye bath, ready to bring natural colour into your life.

house and garden

To start with, reconsider the things you throw into the bin or compost when you're cooking. Onion skins hold an incredible amount of dye colour. Discarded cabbage and kale leaves, carrot tops, ends of beetroot, and pumpkin and squash skins all yield beautiful hues. One of my all-time favourite colours is the soft dusty pink given by avocado rinds and the slightly deeper shade from the pit. You can recycle used tea bags, coffee grounds and the mulch left over from juicing various fruits and vegetables. Even leftover red wine can be used when it's no longer drinkable. This is such a great way to source colour, as you are getting an extra use out of the by-products of your cooking, and you can still put them in the compost afterwards to nourish the land.

If you're lucky enough to have a garden or allotment, then you have an almost limitless opportunity for growing colour. Many herbs, such as rosemary, mint, sage and thyme, give good strong colours. They are also often pretty hardy plants that carry on growing throughout the colder months of the year and so offer an ongoing source of colour. Along with a selection of garden vegetables and herbs, you can also grow various flowers such as roses, daffodils, tulips and hollyhocks for brighter shades and for using with bundle-dyeing and hapazome techniques. You can also buy traditional dye plant seeds and rhizomes (from certified organic sources), such as madder, weld and even indigo, to grow in your garden.

farm and wilderness

If you live near any farms, find out what grows in them and if the farmer would be happy to let you take away any waste produce or invasive weeds. Dock plants are a big nuisance to farmers and most would welcome the opportunity to be relieved of them. Things such as walnut husks are discarded once the walnuts have been removed, and can be recycled to make the most wonderful shades of brown and black.

If you don't have access to a garden or farm, look around at your local landscape. There are endless plants that have colour potential in the wild and natural spaces around us. Where I live, there are hedgerow plants that grow abundantly – such as nettles, blackberries, and apple trees – and other species that are commonly found in woodland, such as bracken and pine. Meadows and lawns are often dotted with outcrops of yarrow, dock and dandelion. Even waste ground can be a great place for finding certain plants and herbs.

When collecting leaves and flowers, gather those that have naturally fallen to the ground. If you do take cuttings from the plant, try not to overharvest from just one part. Take every third leaf/flower on the stem, or gather material from every third plant. And only take from healthy plants that can easily regenerate. You can also collect seeds or take cuttings to propagate from local wild plants.

Always ask the landowner for permission before you forage for any plants, even if it is a public space.

online

For any other type of dye that you cannot grow or source locally, you can go to responsible online suppliers of sustainable natural dyes (see p142). These come as dried dye materials, including wood chips, powders and extract powders. For more on this, see p47.

tips on growing your own garden

Each season brings with it a new palette of colours, whether they are from different parts of a plant, or from entirely different plants. Your choice of plants for your garden will be governed by those that are native to where you are in the world or that grow well in the local soil and climate.

To maximise their usage, consider growing plants that offer a range of properties within themselves: herbs that heal and give colour, and fruit and vegetables that offer nutrition as well as pigments. Focus on planting a good number of self-propagating perennial varieties, which do not need replanting each year. And try growing plants that grow back quickly when cut, such as kale and mint. Also consider having a patch of nettles – they regenerate rapidly and seem to thrive when cut back every now and then. They also offer excellent nitrogen-fixing qualities to enrich your soil. You can also grow natural ingredients for mordants, such as rhubarb, borage or a walnut tree.

It's good to have a mixture of annuals, with a thought to the colours that will be available through each season of the plant's growth cycle. Consider which parts of the plant you will use to extract colour. Can you use the leaves, fruit and nuts, rather than having to dig up the whole plant for its roots? If so, you have a renewable resource at your fingertips. When you're ready to use your plant, consider where its energy is at different times of the year. In the cooler months, the energy is stored in the roots, then it moves up into new leaves. When seeding, the energy and strong colour is in the seeds, and once these dry and fall off, the energy cycles back down into the roots. Go to where the energy of the plant is to obtain its richest colour source.

Aim for a collection of plants that gives you a rainbow of colours to choose from. In temperate climates, you can start by using woad for blue, madder for rich reds, dock and dandelion root for mustard yellows, hollyhocks for dark red, sunflowers for their purple-producing seeds, onions for orange, comfrey for green and meadowsweet for black. Indigo, madder and weld are the traditional three primary colours used to attain a wider range of colours, so consider planting these from seed.

the language of dyeing

Acid (acidic) and Alkali (alkaline) This refers to where a substance sits on the pH-scale. If a substance has a pH level 1–4, it is acidic; if the pH level is 5–7, it is neutral; 8–11 is alkaline. You can test the pH level of a substance using litmus paper.

Alum In this book, alum refers to potassium aluminium sulphate. It is a non-toxic metallic compound that can be used as a mordant to help fix dyes to fibres.

Curing A curing process is often used to help colour set into fibre. To cure a fibre that has been dyed, hang it somewhere dry, out of direct sunlight. Leave it to air dry and cure for a period of time, from several days to weeks, before washing. The longer you leave it, the better the setting results.

Disposal of dyes When working with non-toxic natural dyes in small quantities, you can dispose of remaining dye bath solutions by diluting them with water and flushing them into the sewage system/down the drain. In some cases, you can use the remaining dye bath as feed for certain plants (see 'Disposal of mordants and modifiers'). Those working with larger quantities should use a professional water filtration system to clean their dye water before it goes into the sewage system/down the drain.

Disposal of mordants and modifiers When working with non-toxic mordants (alum, iron and tannin) and modifiers in small quantities, you can dispose of them by diluting with plenty of water and then flushing them into the sewage system/down the drain. Alum and iron mordants can also be poured into the soil near the roots of acid-loving plants such as heather, laburnum, blue spruce and magnolia. If doing so, dilute with lots of water first and pour into different spots around your garden, over a course of time, so as not to affect the pH balance of the soil or damage the plants.

Dye bath A solution of dye pigments suspended in water that is used to dye fibres.

Dye colour To check a dye bath has a deep enough colour, dip a spoon into the bowl: if it disappears and you can't see it under the surface, you have lots of colour.

Dye material The material used for dyeing, such as plant matter (leaf, flower, root, berry, nut, bark), or food waste. This can be fresh or dry, whole or chips/shavings. It covers dye powder and extract powder.

Dye pot A non-reactive vessel used to contain a dye bath. In this book, it is often referred to simply as a 'pot'.

Extract powder A dye powder made up of dye particles that have been isolated and extracted from the original dye material – it is much stronger than standard dye powder. Sometimes referred to as 'dye extract powder'.

Fastness (light, colour, rub, wash) The quality of being fixed and a measure of the resistance of a material or dye to fading caused by exposure to light, rubbing, wear, washing or age.

Fibre In this book, fibre refers to textiles and paper, and their natural substance – e.g. animal fibres for textiles such as silk and alpaca, and plant fibres for textiles such as hemp and cotton. The term 'fabric' is also used throughout the project pages, which is interchangeable with 'cloth'.

Layer dyeing Some dyes work better when colour is built up in layers by dyeing the fibre once, and then again. This is in contrast to using more dye material in a dye bath. Layer dyeing can give longer-lasting and more reliable results.

Modify/modifier Modifiers are solutions used to change the colour of dyes and give a wider range of colours. Dyes are modified to give different colour results.

Mordant A solution used to help dyes bond with fibre for more colourfast results. It also affects the colour outcomes of the dye. It can be used before (pre-mordant), during, or after (post-mordant/after-mordant) the dyeing process. The best results are often obtained from pre-mordanting.

Non-reactive Refers to the material of a dye pot or other piece of equipment that does not react with dyes. Examples include stainless steel, glass and ceramic. In contrast reactive materials such as iron, tin and copper can leach into solutions and cause changes in colour.

Overdyeing Dyeing fibre that has already been dyed, therefore adding another layer of dye colour on top, which may alter the overall shade of the fibre.

pH A numeric scale used to determine the acidity or alkalinity of a water soluble substance.

pH-neutral soap A mild soap with a neutral pH level that is suitable for sensitive skin. Most soaps have an alkaline pH level that can damage skin/fibre and also affect delicate natural dyes and alter colours. It's best practice to use pH-neutral soaps for all natural dyeing processes and to care for naturally dyed fibres as it preserves and lengthens the life of their colours. I like to use Dr Bronner's organic baby unscented liquid soap.

Pre-wet/pre-wetting Before using any textiles (cloth, yarn or fleece) for any natural dyeing process, including mordanting, dyeing and modifying, you should always ensure your fibre is thoroughly wetted. This ensures the fibre particles are open, porous and best able to receive dye/mordant/modifier solutions consistently all over. Do this by soaking the fibre in clean water, ideally for 8 to 12 hours, or at the very least one hour. For full instructions, see p26.

Safety Always take precautions when handling mordant, dye and modifier materials. Use protective goggles to cover eyes, gloves for hands and a dust mask for airways, and work in a well-ventilated area. Do not put any materials in your mouth and keep away from children and animals. Always supervise children.

Sampling Always test a scrap piece of your fibre in the mordant, dye bath or modifier solution in order to check you have the correct solutions to create your desired colour outcomes.

Scour Cloth, yarn, fleece (and all other fibre in this book except paper) should always be scoured prior to any part of the dye process to remove dirt, grease, starches or dust and ultimately achieve good, clear and consistent colours. For full instructions, see p26.

Sustainable Using methods that allow biological systems to remain diverse and healthy, avoiding depletion or permanent damage of natural resources or the environment.

Water This book offers guidelines for the amount of water to use, but no exact measures. This is because the amount of water you need depends on the size of the fibre you are dyeing and the dye pot you are using. You always need to use enough clean water to allow your fibre to move freely. Make sure there is space at the top of the dye pot to allow the dye bath to simmer, boil or be stirred. If at any time in the process you don't have enough water, top up with more clean water at a similar temperature. This won't dilute the dye colour – the same amount of colour remains in the water. Keep an eye on water to maintain suitable levels throughout all processes. The temperature of the water isn't too important, but it's what's comfortable for your hands. There are times when boiling water is necessary, and this has been stated throughout.

Weighing fibre/fabric Many of the dye recipes require you to weigh the fibre. Always do this after it has been washed and scoured and left to dry – you'd be surprised how much dirt will be washed away and how much that dirt weighed.

Wood chips Some wood dyes, such as logwood and sappanwood, can be bought as wood chips. These are made from cutting or chipping larger parts of the wood.

2 fibres, mordants and modifiers

choosing the right fibres

Before starting, consider the most suitable fibre (textile/fabric) for your project. Natural fibres, in their unbleached and undyed state, are the first choice for natural dyeing practices.

Many fibres are bleached to give a pure white colour in place of their natural grey or beige. This renders the natural dyeing process somewhat obsolete, so try to buy unbleached and undyed fibres to work with. Their natural colour provides a good base on which to build and enrich your dye colours. Additionally, try to choose organically grown and sustainable varieties.

Generally, there are two groups of fibres – animal (protein) fibres and plant (cellulose) fibres. Depending on which group the fabric belongs to, the way in which it should be treated and how it responds to the dye process will differ. The following pages give you an overview of the variety of fibres available, and how they pair with various mordants.

a note on sustainable fibres

Using sustainable fibres is key in any environmentally conscious process. Most sustainable fibres come with pros and cons – it's hard to find one that is 100% environmentally and socially positive. Look at the fibre's full life cycle, from the soil it is grown in to the effect it will have when it goes back into the earth at the end of its life cycle. From this informed position you can decide which fibres suit your own priorities.

Many 'eco-fibres', such as bamboo, rayon, viscose and tencel, are made from plant fibres – but they require intensive chemical processing to turn them into fabric. For this reason I choose to avoid them entirely. Petroleum-based synthetic fibres, such as polyester, are derived from oil and do not biodegrade. And, when laundered, acrylic fabrics have been found to release

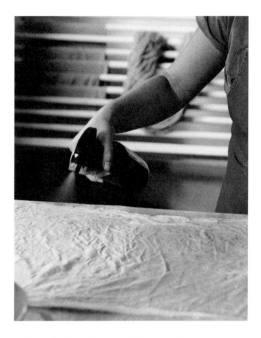

millions of micro-plastic particles into water systems, posing an environmental threat to marine wildlife, as well as entering the food chain. Recycled fibres are made from scraps of textile from factories or post-consumer use, which are spun into thread for making new fabrics. Despite the waste reduction, they can contain synthetic fibres and chemicals so pose the same issues as other artificial fibres.

plant fibres

cotton
linen
hemp
ramie
nettle

Plant fibres require more processing than animal fibres to achieve the same intensity of colour when dyed. They are fairly stubborn at receiving colour so often appear pale unless a mordant is used to help fix the dye. In a sense, we use a mordant to make them act more like animal fibres, and take up the colour better.

Plant fibres are much more resilient to temperature changes and extremes than animal fibres. They can generally be boiled without damage, and taking them rapidly from hot to cold or vice versa does not have such dramatic effects.

a note on recycled paper

Paper can be made from all kinds of plant fibres, from wood, banana and mango plants to cotton and mushrooms. You can look for eco-paper suppliers – one UK company produces paper made using the by-product of corn farming. Recycled paper is usually made from post-consumer waste paper, which means that it is likely to contain varying levels of synthetic pigments and solvents, although it is possible to find recycled paper that has not undergone further chemical bleaching, processing or colouring. Ideally buy your paper from a local mill. Or look for Khadi paper, which is made from post-consumer cotton in India, and has a beautiful soft texture. Do note that it is generally made with bleached cotton and may be mixed with additional synthetic materials.

sustainable plant fibres

Organic cotton This uses fewer chemical pesticides and fertilisers than standard cotton but still requires vast amounts of water to grow and process. If it's grown in rainy countries, this is less of a problem, but many producers are in drought-prone areas and rely on mains water or river water, which then impacts local communities. Sadly, only about 1% of global cotton production uses organic systems.

Linen Made from the flax plant, which requires minimal fertilisers for growing and less pesticide control than cotton. Linen is one of the strongest fibres: it is breathable, highly absorbent and takes dye well compared to other plant fibres.

Hemp A quick-growing bast-fibre plant that provides a fast turnover of crop, and easily provides two to three times more fibre per acre than cotton. It doesn't require herbicides or pesticides because it is naturally pest-tolerant and it enriches the soil by fixing nutrients back into it. As a fabric, hemp is breathable, warm, moisture wicking, anti-bacterial and durable.

Ramie A perennial plant that has been cultivated for its fibre for thousands of years. Native to eastern Asia and belonging to the same family as the nettle, its strong bast fibre reaches very long lengths, making it ideal to spin for textiles. Ramie grows quickly and well without chemical herbicides and pesticides. The task of retting – the removal of the fibre from the plant for processing – is specialist and requires hard manual work, which makes it expensive to produce. When produced by hand ramie is chemical free, but it can also be produced industrially, in which case it's chemically intensive. Ramie is a lustrous fabric, similar to silk, although much stronger.

Nettle This grows abundantly with low maintenance and minimal water in most bio-regions. Nettles grow in the poorest-quality soil without the aid of herbicides or pesticides, and fix nitrogen and other nutrients back into it. Nettle fabric is a soft and lustrous fibre.

animal fibres

> wool
> silk
> alpaca
> mohair

Animal fibres tend to take up dye colours and hold on to them much more successfully than plant fibres and can often be used without a mordant.

But they can be delicate, and need to be treated gently when processing. Use cold or low-temperature dyeing techniques so as not to disrupt the quality of the fibres. Silk can lose its sheen when a high heat is applied, while wool is quick to shrink if exposed to hot temperatures.

It's also important not to shock the animal fibres by taking them from one extreme temperature to another. Instead, let temperature changes happen gradually – allow a dye bath to cool naturally before removing the fibres and washing them in cool water. Similarly, put cold-washed fibres into a cold dye bath and increase the temperature slowly.

sustainable animal fibres

Wool Organic wool is available from a limited number of farmers. In the UK, organic wool comes from sheep that are fed only 100% organic grains, graze on certified organic land, and are not treated with chemical dips or antibiotics. Ideally organic sheep are grazed in rotation with cattle, allowing both animals access to different grasses, which provide wider nutritional value.

Peace silk A lustrous fabric, made from the cocoons of silk worms. For conventional silk the worm is killed by boiling the cocoon, but peace silk, or ahimsa silk, allows the worm to live and hatch out as a moth. This means that the single continuous thread of the cocoon is broken into several pieces when the creature eats its way out. As a result, the fibre requires extra work to spin and is more expensive, but the result is as good as other silk.

Alpaca Made from the fleece of the alpaca, a South American camelid similar to a small llama, alpaca wool is softer than sheep wool, as well as free of lanolin, which makes it hypoallergenic. Alpacas are usually grazed on mountainsides, where they roam freely. Because their rearing generally requires no pesticides or antibiotic treatments, their wool is often naturally organic.

Mohair This comes from the mohair goat. It's silky and strong, with natural flame retardancy and elasticity, and it doesn't felt or crease. The majority of commercial mohair comes from South Africa and the USA. Make sure you source it from small-scale farms using sustainable practices, such as rotational grazing (which encourages soil health) and hand blade-shearing, to improve animal welfare.

fibres, mordants and modifiers

washing and scouring

Before using fibres for dyeing or printing you need to prepare them properly, so that no dust, grease, starch or any kind of dirt that might disrupt the quality of the dye results is hiding within them.

1. First, put the fibre through a 40°C (104°F) wash in the washing machine, or wash by hand if using fibres that are too delicate for machine washing.

2. To scour the fibre, put it straight from the wash – in its damp state – into a large non-reactive pot filled with water. It should be big enough for the fibre to move around freely. It's important not to overload the pot, as the dirt needs to be able to easily escape from the folds of the fibre.

3. Add an ecological soap, which is safe to dispose of and non-irritating to the skin. You'll need a similar amount of soap to what you'd use for your normal laundry load.

4. If using delicate animal fibres such as silk, wool or cashmere, bring the water to a gentle simmer and keep it there for an hour, stirring regularly. Then turn off the heat and leave the fibre to cool in the water.

5. If using sturdier plant fibres such as linen or cotton, bring the water to the boil, and continue to boil for an hour, stirring regularly. Then turn off the heat and leave the fibres to cool in the water.

6. Once everything has cooled, tip away the dirty, soapy water and replace it with clean water to rinse the fibres in by hand. You may need to repeat this two or three times, until the water appears clear of soap suds and dirt.

You can use the fibres right away in their damp state. If you don't need them immediately, hang them out to air dry and then store them in sealed bags or boxes to protect them from moths, dust and dirt until you are ready to use them.

weighing fibre

Many of the dye recipes in this book require you to weigh the fibre. Always do this after it has been washed and scoured and left to dry – you'd be surprised how much dirt will be washed away and how much that dirt weighed.

pre-wetting

Fibres need to be pre-wetted before going into the dye bath. In their damp state the particles that make up the fibre expand, open and become porous, making them better able to receive the solution in which they are submerged. This means they can take up dye, mordant or modifier consistently all over. To pre-wet a fibre, place it in a large pot of water and allow it to soak for at least one hour or, for better results, 8 to 12 hours or overnight. The longer you leave it, the better the outcome.

mordanting/pre-wetting

After mordanting, fibres can be washed, rinsed and wrung to remove excess water. Then, in their damp state, they can be added into the dye bath – no need for further pre-wetting.

But if the mordanted fibre has been allowed to air dry (perhaps for use later), then it will need to be pre-wetted. When you're ready to dye, pre-wet the fibre following the instructions above, and use in its damp state.

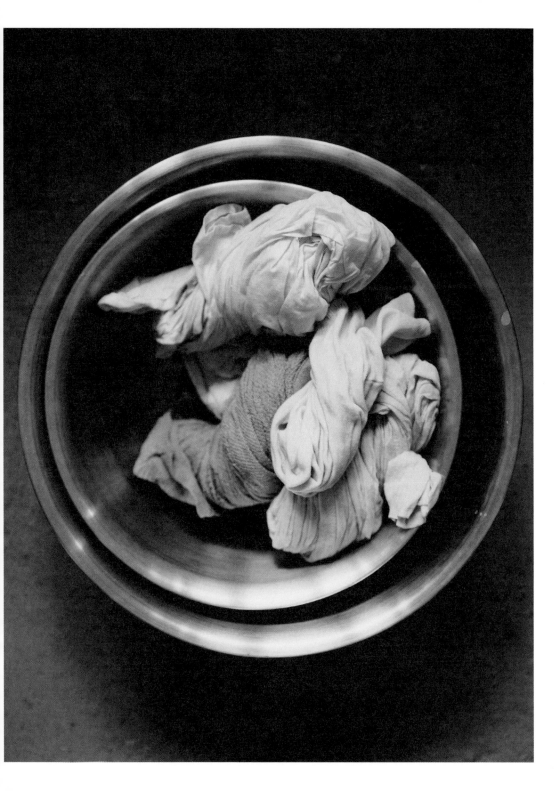

mordants

Most dyes require a fixative, which dyers call a mordant, to help the colours chemically bond with the fibres. The word 'mordant' comes from the Latin word *mordere*, which means 'to bite': the mordant allows the colour to bite into the fibre so it is resistant (fast) to light, washing or rubbing.

Mordanting can be done before, during or after the dyeing process. I recommend 'pre-mordanting' before dyeing for the most reliable and consistent results (except when using iron, which is better as an after-mordant). The type of fibre dictates the kind of mordant you need to use – animal fibres require different mordants from plant fibres.

Mordants also impact the colour of the dye. On the chart on pp58–59 you can see the difference in dye colour that results from using a mineral-based mordant and a plant-based mordant on both animal and plant fibres.

Plant-based mordants are preferable to mineral-based mordants as they are natural, renewable resources, and generally safer to dispose of after use. Their drawback is that they tend to leave a slight beige or yellow tint on fabric prior to dyeing, which can affect the colour outcomes of the dye if you are aiming for pale shades. This often mean deeper hues, which shouldn't be an issue if you are after rich, deep shades, but you might find a light, pale or bright colour such as bubblegum pink or pastel yellow harder to achieve. The colour chart (pp58–59) highlights that you can obtain rich and beautifully muted colours with plant-based mordants.

storing mordants
See p18 for how to dispose of a mordant. Note that you can reserve mordant baths as a base for future mordant making. Store them in lidded buckets or airtight jars in a cool, dark, dry place. To use, top up the remaining mordant with the correct quantity of ingredients based on the weight of your fabric.

The rhubarb mordant (p30) can be kept for up to six months. The alum and cream of tartar mordant (p31) can be kept indefinitely. The oak gall mordant (p33) can also be stored for years. If anything starts to smell, you may prefer to dispose of it.

plant-based mordants
Plant fibres can be mordanted with a plant-based mordant such as tannic acid, which can easily be extracted from oak galls (the most traditional and effective method in the UK), as well as oak bark, chestnuts, acorns, walnuts and other nuts and barks.

Animal fibres can be mordanted with a plant-based mordant such as oxalic acid, which is extracted from rhubarb leaf (also the most traditional and commonly used method in the UK), as well as staghorn sumac, borage and certain seaweeds.

Look at which plant-based mordants you have access to in your local environment before defaulting to mineral-based mordants, which are often either synthetically produced or finite resources (except for homemade iron water, see p39). Avoid using most heavy metals, which are considered toxic, and follow safety precautions when processing any plant mordants that might be toxic, too.

mineral-based mordants
These days mineral-based mordants tend to contain synthetically produced versions of the natural mineral, but at least this means they don't use finite resources.

I only work with iron and alum (potassium aluminium sulphate), as mineral mordants. It's best to avoid using any heavy metals that are considered toxic (such as copper or tin). Alum is considered a non-toxic light metal and iron is a heavy metal that is considered safe to use in small quantities. When used properly in the correct quantities, alum is fully absorbed into fibres so there should be none left in the water that might get flushed down the drain after use. However, you should always dispose of remaining mordant responsibly (see p18).

Alum can be used with both animal and plant fibres but it requires an assistant – or 'assist' – to help the fibres absorb it completely. For plant fibres the assist is soda ash. For animal fibres, cream of tartar is used.

mordants for animal fibres

plant-based mordant
rhubarb leaf

Rhubarb is a perennial plant that regrows each year without the need for replanting. Although the raw leaf is high in oxalic acid, which is toxic, the acid is broken down with heat and therefore non-toxic after it has been extracted with heat and used for mordanting. It can simply be dug into the ground or put on the compost heap after use.

Rhubarb leaf does leave a beige-yellow colour on fabrics when used as a mordant, and this has an effect on the outcome if you are trying to achieve a pale shade: colours may seem a little murky compared to those mordanted with a mineral-based mordant. They are beautiful nonetheless.

plant-based mordant recipe

As this mordant is based on rhubarb leaf (which contains oxalic acid), it's important to work with it in a well-ventilated area, as the fumes are toxic. Protect your hands with gloves and wear a dust mask and eye protectors when working close to the pot.

You will need:
Fibre (washed, scoured and dry)
Rhubarb leaves
Scales
3 large pots, with lids
Strainer
Long-handled spoon
pH-neutral soap

1. Weigh the fibre after it has been washed, scoured and dried. Use 200% of the weight of the fibre in rhubarb leaf. For example, for 100g (3½oz) of fibre, use 200g (7oz) of rhubarb leaf. You should weigh the fibre and calculate the correct weight of rhubarb to use before you begin preparing the mordant.

2. Place the fibre in a large pot of water and allow it to soak for at least one hour, or ideally 8 to 12 hours/ overnight, so that the fibre is pre-wetted.

3. Wash the leaves and chop them up very small so that they are shredded. Put them into another large pot, which should be big enough for them to be completely covered with water.

4. Cover the leaves with boiling water. Bring the water to a simmer, place a lid on the pot and simmer for one hour.

5. After one hour, turn off the heat and leave the pot to cool. Once the solution has cooled, strain out the plant material, reserving the liquid in another large pot with a lid. The pot should be big enough to hold the fibre you want to mordant, and you need to make sure there is enough liquid for the fibre to move around freely so that the mordant can reach all of it consistently. Top up with more warm water if there isn't enough.

6. Add the pre-wetted fibre to the mordant solution. Bring the solution to a simmer, cover with a lid, and simmer for one hour.

7. Stir gently and occasionally with a long-handled spoon. Be sure to tease out any air bubbles trapped under the fibre, as these can make it rise above the surface of the liquid where the mordant cannot reach it properly. Moving the fibre also helps to separate any areas that are touching or in contact with the side of the pot, where the mordant may not be able to reach them.

8. Turn off the heat and allow everything to cool. Once cooled, move the fibre from the solution. Gently wring out excess liquid.

9. Rinse the fibre with cool water, wash it with pH-neutral soap and cool/lukewarm water, then rinse it again to remove the soap.

10. Use the fibre in its damp state and add it to your dye bath. Or hang out the fibre to air dry somewhere warm and dry, out of direct sunlight, for later use.

mineral-based mordant
alum and cream of tartar

Alum (potassium aluminium sulphate) helps to improve the colourfastness of dyes, so they are less likely to fade from light and washing. It also helps to brighten colour tones. It is considered non-toxic in small quantities, so it is safe to use, but it should not be inhaled, ingested or come into contact with skin as it can cause irritation. You can buy it online or from Asian or South American food stores.

Use the exact quantity of alum required for the weight of your fibre, so it is all absorbed by the fibre and not wasted.

Cream of tartar is a synthetic compound that is considered safe enough to use as a food additive. It acts as an 'assist' to help the uptake of the alum by the fibre.

mineral-based mordant recipe

Always work in a well-ventilated area and wear gloves, a dust mask and eye protectors when working with alum-based mordants.

You will need:
Fibre (washed, scoured and dry)
Scales
Alum
Cream of tartar
2 large pots, with lids
Measuring spoons
Heatproof jar
Long-handled spoon
Small lid or plate (optional)
pH-neutral soap

1. Weigh the fibre after it has been washed, scoured and dried. Use 8% of the weight of the fibre in alum, and 7% of the weight of the fibre in cream of tartar. You should weigh the fibre and calculate the correct weight of alum and cream of tartar to use before you begin preparing the mordant.

2. Place the fibre in a large pot of water and allow it to soak for at least one hour, or ideally 8 to 12 hours/overnight, so that the fibre is pre-wetted.

3. Fill a pot with room-temperature water. The pot should be large enough to contain the fibre you want to mordant, sufficient water to cover it, and still provide enough space for the fibre to move freely.

4. Measure out the cream of tartar into a heatproof jar and add enough boiling water for it to dissolve completely when stirred. Then add this to the pot of water, stirring with a long-handled spoon to mix it in.

5. Measure out the alum into the heatproof jar and add enough boiling water for it to dissolve completely when stirred. Then add this to the pot of water, again stirring with a long-handled spoon to mix it in.

6. Add the pre-wetted fibre to the mordant solution. Bring the solution to a simmer, cover with a lid and simmer for one hour.

7. Stir gently and occasionally with a long-handled spoon. Be sure to tease out any air bubbles trapped under the fibre, as these can make it rise above the surface of the liquid where the mordant cannot reach it properly. Moving the fibre also helps to separate any areas that are touching, or in contact with the side of the pot, where the mordant may not be able to reach them.

8. Turn off the heat and allow the fibre to cool in the pot overnight. Then remove the fibre from the pot and gently wring out any excess liquid.

9. Rinse the fibre with cool water, wash with pH-neutral soap and cool/lukewarm water, then rinse again to remove the soap.

10. Use the fibre in its damp state and add it to your dye bath. Or hang it up to air dry somewhere warm and dry, out of direct sunlight, for later use.

mordants for plant fibres

plant-based mordant
oak gall

A simple one-step method for mordanting plant fibres is to use tannic acid extracted from oak galls. Oak galls are small spherical growths that form on oak trees when the gall wasp lays its eggs in the buds of the tree. The tree reacts by growing tissue around the egg, which protects it until it hatches out, leaving behind an escape hole. You should look for this hole when harvesting to ensure that the oak galls you pick do not still have a creature inside. The end of the summer is usually a good time to harvest, or when leaves have fallen off the tree later in the year and the galls are easier to spot. You can also easily buy whole galls or oak gall extract powder for mordanting online. I've used the extract powder in this recipe.

Because of their particularly high tannin content, oak galls are an excellent plant-based mordant for plant fibres. But remember they can leave a beige hue on the fabric.

one-step plant-based mordant recipe

This mordant is based on oak gall (tannic acid). Wear gloves when making this mordant to avoid any irritation.

You will need:
Fibre (washed, scoured and dry)
Scales
2 large pots
Oak gall extract powder
Jar
Long-handled spoon
pH-neutral soap

1. You will need 1 tsp of oak gall extract powder for every 100g (3½oz) of fibre weight after it's been washed, scoured and dried. You should weigh the fibre and calculate the correct weight of gall to use before you begin preparing the mordant.

2. Place the fibre in a large pot of water and allow it to soak for at least one hour, or ideally 8 to 12 hours/ overnight, so that the fibre is pre-wetted.

3. Meanwhile, place the required amount of oak gall powder in a jar and add enough hot water to make a paste. Stir in more hot water to make a solution, allowing the powder to dissolve in the water.

4. Fill a large pot with water; the pot should be big enough for the fibre to be covered with water, with space for it to move around freely.

5. Pour the oak gall mordant solution into the pot and stir it in with a long-handled spoon. Bring to a simmer and simmer for one hour. Turn off the heat and allow the pot to cool to a lukewarm temperature.

6. Take the pre-wetted fibre out of the soaking water, and gently wring out any excess water. Place the fibre in the mordant solution and leave to soak for 8 to 12 hours, stirring occasionally so that the fibre absorbs the mordant consistently all over.

7. Remove the fibre from the solution and gently wring out any excess liquid. Rinse the fibre in lukewarm or cool water, then gently wash it with pH-neutral soap and rinse it again with water to remove the soap.

8. Use the fibre in its damp state and add it to your dye bath. Or hang it up to air dry somewhere warm and dry, out of direct sunlight, for later use.

mineral-based mordant
oak gall with alum and soda ash

A two-step method is the most effective option for saturated, deep and strong, long-lasting dye results on plant-based fibres. Alum, with soda ash as an assist, together help the uptake of dyes, brighten colours and ensure they last longer. You need to follow the oak gall mordant recipe first (see p33), then undertake a second mordanting.

Soda ash (sodium carbonate) was originally obtained from the ashes of certain plants and seaweed. It is now available as a synthetically produced mineral, made from limestone and salt. While it has many purposes, including as an ingredient in baking, eye protectors, gloves and a dust mask should be worn when handling it, as the dust can be an irritant.

For more on alum (aluminium potassium sulphate) see p31. Do note that it should not be inhaled or ingested, or come into contact with skin as it can cause irritation.

two-step mineral-based mordant recipe

This mordant is based on oak gall (tannic acid) plus alum and soda ash. When working with alum and soda ash mordants, always work in a well-ventilated area and wear gloves, dust mask and eye protection.

You will need:
Fibre, prepared with the one-step plant-based recipe
Alum
Heatproof jar
Soda ash
Scales
2 large pots, with lids
Long-handled spoon
pH-neutral soap

1. Weigh the fibre after it has been washed, scoured and dried. You will need 20% of the fibre's weight in alum, and 6% of its weight in soda ash. For example, for 100g (3½oz) fibre, you'll need 20g (½oz) alum and 6g (⅛oz) soda ash. You should weigh the fibre and calculate the correct weight of gall and soda ash to use before you begin preparing the mordant.

2. Follow all the steps of the one-step plant-based mordant recipe (see p33), and once the fibre is hanging to dry, make the alum mordant.

3. Choose a pot that is large enough so that the fibre can be covered with water and move around easily. Half-fill the pot with water.

4. Measure out the alum based on the ratio outlined above. Add to a heatproof jar and pour in enough boiling water to dissolve it. Add to the pot of water.

5. Measure out the soda ash based on the ratio outlined above, and add it to the pot of water.

6. Bring the water to a simmer, stirring to dissolve the soda ash thoroughly. Add more water so that there is enough to cover the fibre, and stir well to mix it.

7. Add the fibre, which will still be damp if you are at the end of the one-step mordanting process. If your fibre is now dry, you'll need to pre-wet it first: place it in a large pot of water and allow it to soak for at least one hour, or ideally 8 to 12 hours/overnight.

8. Heat to a simmer, then turn off the heat and leave to soak for 8 hours, stirring occasionally so that the fibre absorbs the mordant consistently all over.

9. Take the fibre out of the pot and gently wring out any excess liquid. Rinse the fibre with lukewarm or cool water, gently wash it with pH-neutral soap, then rinse it again to remove the soap.

10. Use the fibre in its damp state and add it to your dye bath. Or hang it up to air dry somewhere warm and dry, out of direct sunlight, for later use.

modifiers

After you've mordanted and dyed the fibre, you can use modifiers to extend the range of dye colours further, shifting them to different tones or sometimes entirely new colours altogether.

You can add an acidic or alkaline modifier to a dye bath to change the pH-level. Or you can create a modifier bath in a separate bowl, and add the dyed fabric to it.

acidic modifiers
These tend to shift colours into warmer hues, towards yellow, orange or red. They include citric acid from lemon juice or clear/light vinegar, cranberry juice, tannic acid from oak galls, oxalic acid from rhubarb leaf, dock and sorrel (leaves, stems and roots), cream of tartar and tartaric acid.

alkaline modifiers
These can move colours toward green or pink, or other unexpected shades, and can make colours more murky. They include wood ash, persimmon juice, baking soda, chalk (calcium carbonate), lime (calcium hydroxide), lye (sodium hydroxide) and soda ash (sodium carbonate). It can be interesting to use iron to modify colours to achieve black or dark hues that are otherwise difficult to achieve with dyes alone.

These generalisations are not applicable to all dyes, as some can react in quite unexpected ways.

using a modifier
There are two basic methods for using a modifier.

Add modifier solution directly to the dye bath
1. Allow the dye bath to cool to room temperature. Mix the required amount of modifier (usually 1–2 tsp or a jarful, or see p38 for exact measures) directly into the dye bath. The dyed fibre should still be in the dye bath.

2. Gently move the fibre around, allowing the modifier to penetrate evenly all over. Open any folds and tease out any air bubbles that may cause the fibre to float above the surface.

3. Leave for several minutes to allow the colour to change. If a more dramatic colour change is required, leave to soak in the modifier for longer. Alternatively, repeat the above steps, adding more of the modifier solution.

4. Remove the fibre, wash with pH–neutral soap, rinse, wring to remove excess liquid, and hang to air dry out of direct sunlight.

Add dyed fibre to a separate modifier bath
1. Allow the dye bath and fibre to cool. Fill a separate bowl with cool/warm water. Mix in the required amount of modifier (usually 1–2 tsp or a jarful, or see p38 for exact measures).

2. Remove the fibre from the dye bath, wring to remove excess dye solution and place in the modifier bath. Gently move the fibre around, allowing the modifier to penetrate evenly all over. Open any folds and tease out any air bubbles that may cause the fibre to float above the surface.

3. Leave for several minutes to allow the colour to change. If a more dramatic colour change is required, leave to soak in the modifier for longer. Alternatively, repeat the above steps, adding more of the modifier solution.

4. Remove the fibre, wash with pH–neutral soap, rinse, wring to remove excess liquid, and hang to air dry out of direct sunlight.

Applying heat
If you're using plant fibres, you can apply heat to the modifier bath for 5 to 10 minutes to speed up the process. You can do the same for animal fibres and acidic modifiers. However, animal fibres are sensitive to alkaline modifiers, so it's best not to apply heat to avoid damage.

A piece of cloth showing true dye colour (dock) in the middle. The top has been dipped in alkaline modifier (soda ash), the bottom has been dipped in acidic modifier (vinegar)

modifier recipes

acidic modifiers

See p36 for guidelines on how to use these modifiers.

Lemon juice or vinegar Use 1–2 tsp per 250g (9oz) of fibre.

Tannic acid from oak galls See recipe on p33. Use 1–2 tsp of the solution per 250g (9oz) of fibre.

Oxalic acid from rhubarb/dock leaf or sorrel leaf, root or stem See recipe on p30. Use 1–2 tsp of the solution per 250g (9oz).

Cream of tartar Dilute ½ tsp in just enough water to dissolve, and make a solution. Then use 1–2 tsp of the solution per 250g (9oz) of fibre.

Tartaric acid Dilute ½ tsp in just enough water to dissolve, and make a solution. Then use 1–2 tsp of the solution per 250g (9oz) of fibre.

alkaline modifiers

Wood ash solution You can easily make your own wood ash solution for use as an alkaline modifier.

You will need:
Wood ash from a wood burner, fire pit or fireplace
2 plastic buckets or containers
Cheesecloth (optional)

1. Remove the cold ashes, making sure they only contain wood ash. Place in a plastic bucket and fill with cold water. Leave to soak for one week, or until the liquid yellows and thickens.

2. Pour off the top level of liquid only into a separate bucket, leaving the bottom layer of sediment behind, or pour all the liquid through a cheesecloth to strain it.

3. Mix half a cup or jam jar of wood ash solution into a bowl of clean water – make sure there is enough liquid for the fibre to move around. This will create an alkaline modifier. To use this, you can simply lift your dyed fibre directly out of its dye bath, wring to remove any excess liquid, and add to the wood ash solution.

4. Alternatively, leave your fibre in the dye bath and allow the bath to cool. Then mix half a cup or jar of wood ash solution directly into the dye bath – this should be enough for a large dye bath and 200–500g (7–18oz) of fibre.

5. In either case, soak the fibre for five to 30 minutes, or until the desired shade has been reached. Turn constantly to allow the modifier solution to reach all areas of the fibre.

6. Remove the fibre and rinse it. Wash it with a pH-neutral soap and rinse it again, then hang it out to air dry.

iron powder (ferrous sulphate) solution

Iron can be used as an alkaline modifier after the dyeing process to create darker tones – or sometimes black – and also as a mordant to improve colourfastness. It can be bought online as a powder.

When working with iron, be sure to keep a separate set of equipment to avoid contamination of other natural dye processes and projects.

Be careful when handling iron powder – it's caustic so it's advisable to wear a dust mask, gloves and eye protectors.

You will need:
Scales
Iron powder (ferrous sulphate)
Old cup or jar
Bowl, spoon and tongs

1. Weigh the dry dyed fibre and note the weight. Then place the fibre in a large pot of water and allow it to soak for at least one hour, or ideally 8 to 12 hours/overnight, so that the fibre is pre-wetted.

2. Calculate 2% of the weight of the dry fibre – this figure will be the quantity of iron powder you need.

3. Put the iron powder into an old cup or jar and add hot water. Stir until dissolved.

4. Fill a bowl with cool/lukewarm water, enough for the fibre to move around in. Add the cup of iron water solution and stir in.

5. While it is still damp from dyeing, place the fibre into the bowl and make sure it is fully submerged. Soak for five to 30 minutes, turning constantly, until a dark enough shade is reached.

6. Remove the fibre and rinse it. Wash it with a pH-neutral soap and rinse it again, then hang it out to air dry.

homemade iron water
If you prefer to make your own source of iron, rather than using ferrous sulphate, you can use the following recipe.

You will need:
Rusty nails, or other small rusty iron objects
Sealable jar, and similarly sized pot
Clear vinegar

1. Place the small rusty metal objects inside a sealable jar. Pour in one part water and two parts vinegar to cover the objects. Seal the lid closed so it is airtight.

2. Once a day, pour the vinegar water out of the jar and into the other pot, leaving the rusty objects in the first jar. Leave the top of the jar open so they are exposed to air.

3. The next day, pour the same vinegar back into the jar with the rusty objects.

4. Continue to do this for one or two weeks, until the liquid has turned a rusty orange colour.

5. When it's ready to use, add one part iron water solution to one part clean water in a large bowl. Make sure there is enough liquid for the dyed fibre to move around in.

6. Soak the fibre for five to 30 minutes until a dark enough shade has been reached. Turn constantly to allow the modifier solution to get to all areas of the fibre.

7. Remove the fibre and rinse it. Wash it with a pH-neutral soap and rinse it again, then hang it out to air dry.

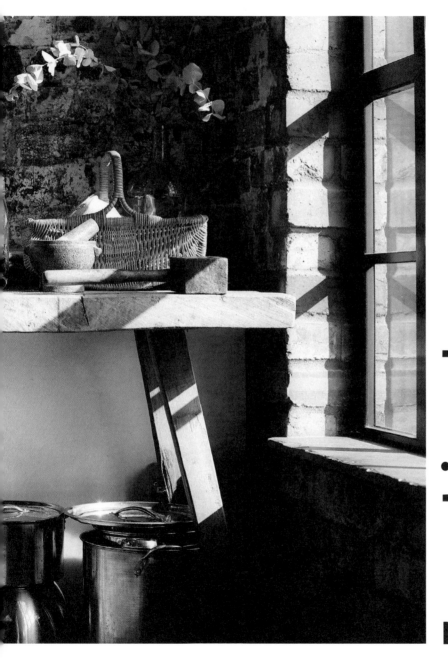

3 making dyes

equipment

separate equipment

Most of the equipment used in dyeing is fairly familiar and found in most homes. However, it's best to reserve a completely separate set of pots, spoons and other equipment for dyeing only. This is particularly important when working with iron – any equipment used with iron should also be kept separate from your other dyeing equipment as it can change dye colours.

non-reactive equipment

It's vital that all the equipment you use for natural dye processes is non-reactive. Stainless steel, heatproof glass and ceramic are the most reliable options. Reactive materials such as copper, tin and iron will react with dyes and cause colour changes. Throughout the book, all equipment listed refers to non-reactive options only.

steaming equipment

Steaming a dyed fibre helps to set the colour (for bundle dyeing, hapazome and block printing). If you have access to a professional fabric steamer or bullet steamer in a textile design studio, use it. I use a textile bullet steamer, but a vegetable or rice steamer may also work as long as you don't mix it up with your kitchen equipment. Alternatively, you can fashion a makeshift steamer out of a stainless steel pot, lid and pasta insert/sieve/colander or cookie cooling rack. If this isn't possible, you can use a regular steam iron with a press cloth to protect the fibre.

A basic natural dye studio will require:

Natural dye powder, extract powder, wood chips or other fresh or dried dye plant material
Mordants
Modifiers
Dye pots – large pots and pans
Large and small mixing bowls
Long-handled spoons
Tablespoons/teaspoons
Measuring spoons
Heatproof measuring jug
Sharp knives
Tongs
Sieve/strainer
Funnel
Pestle and mortar
Blender/food processor/coffee grinder
Scales
Calculator
Heat source – hot plate/stove
Iron
Ironing surface/table
Sealable jars
Lidded plastic storage buckets
Buckets and large plastic tubs
Airtight/sealable plastic boxes and plastic bags
Labels
Pens/pencils/ruler
Cleaning sponges and towels
pH-neutral soap
Eco laundry detergent or washing-up liquid
Rubber/protective gloves
Dust mask
Protective tablecloths
Apron
Protective eyewear
Gardening gloves
Scissors/secateurs
Gathering basket/foraging apron

types of dye

Not all dyes bond with fibres in the same way – some fix to fibres readily with good colourfast results, but most require a little help from a mordant.

So as well as choosing the right fibre for your project, you should also consider the type of dye that will work best for your project. In the Dye Colours chapter (see p56), I've listed the type of dye each dye material produces.

adjective dyes
These dyes won't fix to fibres well without the help of a mordant. When used in conjunction with a mordant, they will bond with fibres much better to produce long-lasting results. Examples include bracken, cochineal and nettle.

substantive dyes
These dyes have naturally occurring fixative chemicals, such as tannins, which work as natural mordants, allowing the dye to fix to the fibre. You can use substantive dyes with a mordant to improve results, but it's not always necessary. Examples include eucalyptus and various tree barks such as oak, apple and cherry.

vat dyes
Unlike all other dyes, these are not soluble in water. The most obvious example is indigo, which is instead soluble in an alkaline environment from which the oxygen has been removed. It requires a slightly more complex process to achieve its beautiful hues, which you can find out about on pp108–115. You don't need a mordant with indigo, as the colour fixes to the fibres with colourfast results.

fugitive dyes
These are not really dyes in the true sense. They are merely stains, which lose colour, change or fade with time. They come from fresh or dried plant material such as flowers, beetroot, turmeric and blackberries. You can't pair them with a mordant to fix to fibres, so just simply embrace their ephemeral quality.

*From top left: Madder powder and dried madder root; Madder powder being turned into a paste;
Adding water to madder powder; Madder powder dye bath*

making a dye bath

The term 'dye bath' is used to describe the dye solution or liquid that has been made using dye material. It is the extracted dye colour suspended in water.

general dye bath-making tips
Dye material quantities Animal fibres take up dye colour more readily than plant fibres, so use slightly more dye material when dyeing plant fibres.

If you are unsure how much fresh dye plant material to use for your quantity of fibre, a ratio of 1 part plant material to 1 part fibre is a good starting point.

Each dye bath requires slightly different quantities of dye material – some guidelines are listed in the Dye Colours chapter on p56. However, the depth and quality of colour from your dye material will vary depending on where and when it was grown, the weather, climate, type of soil, time of year it was harvested and so on. It's therefore hard to predict or replicate exact colours.

Dye bath-making methods If you're unsure about how to turn a dye plant material into a dye bath, remember that most material will release colour if simmered in water for one hour. If a cold extraction is preferred, cover the material with boiling water to activate the process, leave for a few moments, then top with enough water to allow your fibre to move freely. Then leave for several days or weeks, or until a good depth of colour has been achieved.

Adding water to the dye bath The quantity of water used to make a dye bath isn't exact – you simply need enough for the fibre to move around in. You won't reduce the amount of colour in the dye bath by adding water. The same amount of colour remains for the fibre to absorb.

As a guideline, you'll need about 4–5 litres (1 gallon) of water in the dye bath for 100g (3½oz) of fibre. You need enough for the fibre to move around freely so that the dye can reach all of it consistently and evenly. If you realise you don't have enough water after you've made the dye bath, simply top up.

bought materials
Dry dye materials can easily be bought online as wood chips and shavings, dye powder, extract powder, root, bark, insects and petals. Dye powder is simply dye material ground into powder, whereas extract powder is made up of dye particles that have been isolated and extracted from the original dye material – it is much stronger than standard dye powder.

dye powder or extract powder
About 1 tsp of dye powder or extract powder is enough to dye about 100g (3½oz) of washed, scoured and dried animal or plant fibre. But this can vary as natural dyeing isn't an exact science – you'll get the hang of quantities with experience and by using the recipes in this book.

1. Add the powder to a small bowl then add a few drops of hot water to make a paste. Mix well and work out lumps. Then slowly add more water to the paste until you have a liquid.

2. Once you have a liquid solution and the powder is thoroughly blended in, transfer it to the pot you will be dyeing in. Then pour in a few cups of warm water. Stir well to mix and evenly disperse the dye in the water.

3. Add enough water to allow the fibre to move freely. This is your dye bath. Choose your dye bath method on pp52–53.

wood chips and shavings
You'll need about half the weight of the washed, scoured and dried fibre in wood chips. So if you have 100g (3½oz) of fibre, you'll need 50g (1¾oz) of chips.

1. Pour boiling water to just cover the chips. Then top up with enough water so your fibre can move freely.

2. Simmer for 1–2 hours, then leave to soak overnight.

3. Strain and reserve the chips for another future use. This creates your dye bath. Next, you can choose your dye bath method on pp52–53.

found materials

Making dyes from natural materials is so simple. It's like brewing tea – chop the material into small pieces, then steep it in water. You can extract colour from pretty much anything that grows around you. Some colours may be more enchanting than others, but each has its charm.

If you can't forage or grow fresh dye materials, you can also buy them dried. Fresh material often yields brighter results.

leaves

Leaves that work well include nettle, bracken and oak tree. You can also try waste food such as carrot tops and spinach, as well as herbs such as mint. Try to use leaves that have already fallen to the ground, but any fresh, dry or frozen leaves are fine too.

Use a ratio of 1 part leaves to 1 part washed, scoured and dry animal fibre, or a ratio of 2 parts leaves to 1 part washed, scoured and dry plant fibre.

1. Chop the leaves into shreds – the smaller you can chop them the better, as this creates a larger surface area for the colour to escape into the water.

2. Add them to your dye pot. Just cover with boiling water. Wait a few moments and then fill the dye pot with enough warm water to allow the fibre to move around freely.

3. Leave to soak for 1–3 days, or until the water has turned a deep shade. Alternatively, apply heat for around 30 minutes.

4. Strain the leaves and use the liquid as the dye bath.

fresh flowers

Flowers that work well include hollyhocks, marigolds and roses.

Use a ratio of 1 part flowers to 1 part washed, scoured and dry animal fibre. And a ratio of 2 parts flowers to 1 part washed, scoured and dry plant fibre.

You can extract colour from flowers by freezing them – see p103 for the full method. Or use the flowers as part of a bundle dyeing process, see pp96–101 for the full method. Alternatively:

1. Add the flowers to a bowl of warm water (enough to allow the fibre to move around freely) and leave to soak overnight.

2. The next day, simmer the flower mixture for 30 minutes. Then leave to cool.

3. Strain out the flowers and use the liquid as the dye bath.

roots

Roots that work well include dandelion, dock and madder. You can use these fresh or dried.

Use a ratio of 3 parts roots to 1 part washed, scoured and dry animal or plant fibre.

1. If using fresh roots, scrub well to remove any mud. Chop them up into tiny chunks, so that you have the maximum amount of surface area for the dye to escape into the dye bath. Add to your dye pot.

2. Just cover with boiling water. Wait a few moments, then fill the dye pot with enough warm water to allow the fibre to move around freely.

3. Leave to soak for 1–3 weeks, or until the water has turned a deep shade. Alternatively, apply heat for 1–2 hours.

4. Strain the roots and use the liquid as the dye bath.

nuts or bark

Nuts that work well include acorns, chestnut hulls and walnut husks. The best barks include apple (or those of any fruit tree) and oak.

Use a ratio of 3 parts nuts or bark to 1 part washed, scoured and dry animal or plant fibre.

1. Chop the nuts or bark into small pieces; if not possible, leave whole. Add to the dye pot.

2. Just cover with boiling water, wait a few moments, then fill the dye pot with enough warm water to allow the fibre to move around freely.

3. Leave to soak for 1–3 weeks. When a good colour has been reached, simmer the nut/bark mixture for 1 hour. Alternatively, don't soak and simply apply heat for around 1–2 hours.

4. Strain the nuts/bark and use the liquid as the dye bath.

berries

Berries that work well include blackberries, blueberries and elderberries.

Use a ratio of 1 part berries to 1 part washed, scoured and dry animal or plant fibre.

1. In a dye pot, crush the berries to a pulp with a spoon. Cover with enough warm water to allow the fibre to move freely.

2. Place the lid on the dye pot and simmer the berry mixture for 1 hour.

3. Strain the liquid, being careful not to squash/push any of the berry fibre through the sieve. Use the liquid as the dye bath.

food waste

Certain food waste is covered in the methods above. You could also try leftover red wine, which is a ready-made dye. Use it as it is – simply add your fibre before using a hot or cold dyeing method, see pp52–53.

For peel (such as squash, beet, pumpkin, carrot and aubergine peel), follow the avocado dye bath recipe on p67.

tea leaves or coffee grounds

1. Use a ratio of 1 part dye material to 1 part fibre.

2. Just cover with boiling water, wait a few moments, then fill the dye pot with enough water for the fibre to move freely.

3. Leave to soak for 1–3 weeks. Alternatively, simmer for 30–60 minutes.

4. Strain and use the liquid as your dye bath.

Shredding eucalyptus leaves

Eucalyptus leaves being picked, and steeping in a dye pot

dye bath methods

Once you have made the dye bath, there are various ways to dye the fibre – primarily, you can use either a cold dyeing or a hot dyeing method. Where possible I always encourage using a cold dyeing method as it doesn't require an energy source.

Animal fibres These take up dye colours easily and quickly. They are sensitive to heat, so tend to work well with cold dyeing or very gentle heat. Silk is likely to lose its sheen at high temperatures, and wool is likely to shrink. Keep them at or below a simmer, and do not allow to boil. If you are using a cold dyeing method with animal fibres, it's best to use a strong dye bath with a higher percentage of dye material than you might require for hot dyeing.

Plant fibres These are a little more stubborn in taking up colour. But they are much sturdier than animal fibres, so a hot dyeing method is a good option.

For more on animal and plant fibres, and the best way to prepare them for dyeing, see the Fibres, Mordants and Modifiers chapter on p20.

cold dyeing method

1.   Add the pre-mordanted and pre-wetted fibre to the dye bath, with the liquid at a cool or room temperature.

2.   Leave to soak for 1–3 weeks, checking on the colour progress each day, until you have achieved the desired depth of colour. Remember that colours appear lighter once washed and dried.

3.   Reserve the dye bath for another use if there is still colour in it. You can keep dye in a lidded bucket or sealed glass jar for several weeks. If mould appears, simply skim it off before dyeing. Alternatively, you can freeze the dye in a plastic box.

4.   Rinse the fibre in lukewarm water, wash it with a pH-neutral soap, then rinse it again. Hang it to air dry, away from direct sunlight.

If this process doesn't work well for you, you can return the washed fibre (damp) back into the dye bath and follow the hot dyeing method opposite.

hot dyeing method

1.   Add the pre-mordanted and pre-wetted fibre to the dye bath. Slowly raise the temperature of the dye bath to a simmer.

2.   Simmer for 1 hour, gently stirring to allow the dye to reach all parts of the fibre – open up any folded areas or sections that may be touching other areas of the fibre or the sides or bottom of the pot. Tease out any air bubbles trapped in the fibre causing it to rise above the surface.

3.   Leave the fibre to sit in the dye bath overnight, and allow it to cool and the colour to saturate. Remove the fibre and gently wring out any excess dye liquid.

4.   Reserve the dye bath for another use if there is still colour in it. You can keep dye in a lidded bucket or sealed glass jar for several weeks. If mould appears, simply skim it off before dyeing. Alternatively, you can freeze the dye in a plastic box.

5.   Rinse the fibre in lukewarm water, wash it with a pH-neutral soap, then rinse it again. Hang it to air dry, away from sunlight.

solar dyeing
If you live somewhere hot, or during warmer seasons, you can use a solar oven to take advantage of the natural heating rays of the sun. Use a glass jar with a lid – ideally a dark coloured one, which will absorb the sun's heat best, although you can also use a clear glass jar.

1.   Place the fibre in the jar and fill it with the dye liquid. Seal shut with the lid.

2.   Place the jar on a window ledge or outside in direct sunlight. Leave it for several days or weeks, until the desired colour is achieved.

all-in-one dyeing

This method combines fresh dye plant material (leaves, bark, berries and such like) with the fibre.

1. Place the dye plant material in a large pot and cover with boiling water. Leave to soak for 1 hour. Fill with more warm water, so there is enough for the fibre to move freely.

2. After the material has soaked, leave it in the water (do not strain). Then follow the cold or hot dyeing method opposite.

3. Gently stir the pot regularly to keep the dye material from sticking to certain areas of fibre and creating patches of deeper colour. Alternatively, you can exploit this to create a special pattern effect, and do less stirring!

layer dyeing/building colour

If you've dyed the fibre but want a deeper colour, follow these steps:

1. Allow the dye bath to cool, then remove the dyed fibre from the bath. Wash the dyed fibre with pH-neutral soap, then rinse with lukewarm/cool water.

2. Add another 1 tsp of dye or extract powder to the bath and stir to mix. If you're using additional dye plant material, steep it again, then strain out additional material. Then return the still-damp fibre to the dye bath to repeat the dye process.

Most fibres dye better using a multi-stage dye process, so it's good practice to layer-dye like this, building the colour up until you reach the desired shade, rather than over-saturating the first dye bath with dye material.

For darker shades, you can mordant the fibre for a second time after it's been dyed. Then layer-dye as above.

1. Wash the dyed fibre with pH-neutral soap, then rinse with lukewarm/cool water.

2. While the fibre is still damp, follow the relevant mordanting steps (p28). If the dyed fibre is dry, pre-wet (p26) before following the mordanting steps.

3. Return the damp fibre to the dye bath and repeat the dye process.

Madder powder dye bath with silk

yarn and paper

yarn dyeing

If not already in one, start by winding your yarn into a skein to ensure it can soak up the dye well to achieve a consistent colour all over. Use a windmill-style skein winder, a niddy-noddy, a tabletop winder or umbrella swift to do this if you have access to any of them. Otherwise the back of a chair or your forearm will do. Make sure any equipment you use is thoroughly clean before you start, and wind loosely, so you can easily remove the skein afterwards. Once wound, tie it loosely in four places, using a figure-of-eight fastening, which allows the yarn to move freely within the tie. You can then remove the skein from the winder. Doing all this properly prevents the yarn from twisting and knotting in the pot, so is well worth the effort.

1. Wash and scour the yarn (p26), but be careful not to go over a simmer to avoid shrinking the fibre.

2. Prepare the yarn with a mordant. Use a plant-based mordant for strong and earthy colours, or a mineral-based one for brighter tones – see pp28–34. Yarn has a tendency to float, so it's important to make sure all areas of it are equally submerged and receiving the mordant. Try weighing it down with a small and non-reactive lid or plate. This also applies when it's in the dye bath.

3. Pre-wet the yarn by placing it in a large pot of water and allow it to soak for at least 1 hour, or ideally 8 to 12 hours/overnight.

4. Place the pre-wetted yarn into the dye bath. The dye pot should be large enough to let the yarn sit in without being squashed, and there should be enough liquid to cover it. Add more water, if needed.

5. Apply gentle heat. Be sure not to go above a simmer with delicate animal fibres, and not to shock the fibres by moving them between extreme temperatures.

6. Avoid agitating animal fibre yarns such as wool too much, as it can result in felting and fluffing. Simply let the yarn sit in the dye bath for 30 minutes and then turn it over and let it sit for another 30 minutes.

7. If you want a longer dye time than 1 hour, allow half the desired time for each side. This should also help to achieve all-over coverage, as some yarns, especially woollens, tend to float to the surface of the dye pot.

8. Once you have achieved the desired depth of colour, turn off the heat. Leave the yarn in the dye pot to cool and saturate overnight.

9. After removing the yarn from the dye pot, it can be gently rinsed and washed with a pH-neutral soap and lukewarm water. Gently wring out any excess water and hang out the skein to air dry.

paper dyeing

1. Create a dye bath in a non-reactive shallow tray or dish – ceramic or glass is fine. It should be big enough to allow the paper to lie flat.

2. Lay the sheet of paper in the tray and tease it under the surface of the dye bath for a few seconds to absorb the colour. Don't leave the paper submerged in the liquid for a long period of time, as this could cause it to deteriorate and fall apart.

3. If you don't have a shallow tray, you can also use a large dye pot and lower the sheet into it vertically, again taking it out after a few seconds.

4. Air dry the paper by hanging it on a line with a couple of clips or pegs.

5. You can layer the dye by repeating the dye process after the first layer of colour has dried. This will allow the colour to deepen, without compromising the integrity of the paper.

6. Alternatively, you can apply dye colour to paper by brushing it on with a wide, flat brush. Apply a layer of colour, hang it to air dry, and then apply further layers of colour to achieve deeper shades.

Undyed yarn (left); yarn dyed with onion skin (right)

4 dye colours

fibre   mordanted fibre   sappanwood   cochineal   madder   avocado   red dock

Wool with
rhubarb leaf
mordant

Silk with
rhubarb leaf
mordant

Wool with
alum + cream
of tartar
mordant

Silk with
alum + cream
of tartar
mordant

Cotton with
oak gall
mordant

Linen with
oak gall
mordant

Cotton with
oak gall, alum
+ soda ash
mordant

Linen with
oak gall, alum
+ soda ash
mordant

Dyes not pictured: cutch, common hawthorne, marigold and dyer's coreopsis

sappanwood

Sappanwood (*Caesalpinia sappan*), also known as Indian redwood, is a small, thorny, flowering tree from the Fabaceae legume family, which is native to Asia.

It's used in folk medicine (often as a pink drink made with ginger, cinnamon and cloves), and it's long been used for its antimicrobial and anti-allergenic properties: it's believed to protect against skin and joint infections, and food poisoning.

colour
The heartwood of the tree produces beautiful shades of pink and peachy pink through to bright reds and purply reds. It is much lighter in hue than its relation brazilwood (*Paubrasilia*), which you should avoid using as it is an endangered species.

source
Source sappanwood dye from responsibly managed plantations in Asia. Sappanwood is generally available as a dye powder, an extract powder or as wood chips.

type of dye/mordant *Adjective dye*
Use the mordant that best suits the fibre you're dyeing. Sappanwood has poor light-fastness, so avoid using on a dye project that will be exposed to sunlight, such as clothes. Its wash- and rub-fastness is good, and the colour holds well.

making a dye bath
Extract powder
Weigh the fibre after it has been washed, scoured and dried. For a red, use 20% of the weight of the fibre in extract powder – for example, for 400g (14oz) of fibre, use 80g (3oz) of extract powder. For deep reds, use 50–100% of the weight of the fibre in extract powder.

See p47 for how to make an extract powder dye bath.

Wood chips
Weigh the fibre after it has been washed, scoured and dried. For a red, use 25% of the weight of the fibre in chips – for example, with 400g (14oz) fibre, use 100g (3½oz) chips. For a light red, use 10% of the weight of the fibre.

Add the chips to the dye pot and add enough boiling water to allow the fibre to move freely. Leave to soak overnight.

The next day, add a little more water to the pot and boil for 2–3 hours. Leave to sit again overnight before using.

Strain through a piece of muslin and use the liquid as the dye bath. Save the chips for soaking another time.

Dye powder
Weigh the fibre after it has been washed, scoured and dried. Use the same quantities of powder as wood chips (see above).

Add to a small bowl. Add a little water to turn the powder into a paste. Add a little more water to create a solution. Transfer to a dye pot. Fill the pot with enough boiling water to allow the fibre to move freely. Leave to soak overnight.

The next day, add a little more water to the pot and boil for 2–3 hours. Leave to sit again overnight before using as a dye bath.

dye bath method
Suitable with a hot dyeing method. See pp52–53 and follow the additional guidelines below.

For a dye bath made with extract powder, simmer the fibre in the dye bath for 1 hour, stirring gently from time to time. Leave overnight to cool.

For a dye bath made with powder or chips, bring the dye bath to a simmer for 30 minutes to 1 hour.

If the dye results are orangey, you can add chalk powder (calcium carbonate) to the dye bath for a better pink/red.

Add 1 tsp per 100g (3½oz) of fibre.

You can use the dye bath a second time to dye another fibre a peachy pink, or a third time for a pale pink.

modifier
Sappanwood is very pH-sensitive. It will react to acids by turning orange, and to alkalines by turning purple.

cochineal

Cochineal (*Dactylopius coccus*) is a scale insect indigenous to South and Central America, but also introduced to Spain, North Africa and Australia. It is thought to have been harvested by the Aztecs and Mayans, and was once considered more precious than gold. A range of paintings and textiles found preserved in various ancient Mayan and Aztec pyramid tombs feature cochineal, while Aztec women stained their teeth with the crushed insects to appear more attractive.

The insects live on and feed off the nopal cactus (prickly pear) and contain high levels of carminic acid as a natural defence against potential predators, which do not like the acidic taste. It's the female insect and eggs that are used to produce the colour, as they have much higher levels of carminic acid than the males – up to 17–24% of their body mass. The insects are collected individually by hand and then dried and crushed.

colour
Cochineal offers intense hues of scarlet, orange red and bright pink. Depending on the method used to dry the insects, a number of different colours can be achieved, which is why the shades of red vary so much across commercial suppliers. Cochineal can also be used to overdye indigo to get wonderful colourfast purples, or over madder to get a stronger red.

source
Cochineal can be bought online either as whole dried insects or as a dye powder or extract powder, and tends to be imported from Peru.

type of dye/mordant *Adjective dye*
Use the mineral-based alum and cream of tartar mordant to bring out a crimson tone (see p31). Otherwise use the mordant that best suits the fibre you're dyeing.

making a dye bath
Weigh the fibre after it has been washed, scoured and dried, then follow the correct quantities below.

Dye powder
For a deep red, use 20–50% of the weight of the fibre in dye powder – for example, for 400g (14oz) of fibre, use 80–200g (3oz–7oz) of dye powder. About 5% gives a rich pink; and around 1% gives a light pink. Use the same quantities with whole dried cochineal ground into powder.

Extract powder
For a deep red, use 4% of the weight of the fibre in extract powder – for example, for 400g (14oz) of fibre, use 16g (⅓oz) of extract powder.

See p47 for how to make a dye powder and extract powder dye bath, and follow steps 1 to 3.

Once you have made the dye bath, leave it overnight. The next day, add a little more water and bring to a simmer for 15–20 minutes, keeping it below a boil.

If using whole cochineal, you may need to strain through a fine sieve or muslin. Use the liquid as the dye bath.

dye bath method
Suitable with either the cold dyeing or hot dyeing method. See pp52–53 and follow the additional guidelines below.

Cochineal is best used with soft water – hard water has a higher level of impurities, which the carmine bonds to, giving paler dye results. So if you live in a hard water area, use rainwater or distilled water for dyeing.

For the cold dye, leave to sit overnight in the dye bath. For the hot dye, apply a low heat for about 40 minutes.

After taking the fibre out of the dye bath, allow to cure for a couple of days before washing.

After you've dyed the fibre, you can use the dye bath a second or third time to dye another fibre a lighter pink.

modifier
Cochineal is very pH-sensitive. An acidic modifier shifts colours to orange and red. An alkaline modifier shifts hues to plum and purple.

madder

the two separate dyes in madder, alizarin and purpurin, and later discovered anthraquinone, which allowed for a red pigment to be synthesised from coal tar to replace madder dye.

The plant is a small, evergreen, perennial shrub, growing up to 1.2m (4ft) tall, with pale yellow flowers. It likes to grow in rich, deep, well-drained soil, does well in wasteland and hedgerows, and is ready to harvest after three years once the green top has died back in autumn. High-alkaline soil encourages more pigment production in the roots. There are a few kinds of madder you may come across: common madder (*Rubia tinctorum*), wild madder (*Rubia peregrina*) and Indian madder (*Rubia cordifolia*). All can be used for natural dyeing, though Indian madder is less strong in colour and considered inferior.

colour
Madder produces a range of different reds, from orangey red to scarlet and brick red. The colour outcome depends largely on how the madder was grown and processed, the quality of the soil and the age of the root. It also depends on how much of it you add to the dye bath, the type of water you have access to (hard or soft) and the level of heat applied to the dye bath.

source
You can buy madder online as dried root, or dye powder. But it's easy to grow and can be used fresh or dried. The red-brown roots that grow up to 1m (3ft) long are the part that's harvested for dyeing. If you use fresh roots, wash them and then put them aside to dry and cure for a couple of months before grinding them down into a powder. You'll need about 1kg (2.2lb) of fresh madder to yield about 150g (5¼oz) of dried madder.

type of dye/mordant *Adjective dye*
You can achieve an aubergine shade by using a mineral-based mordant on your fibre before dyeing, and an iron solution as an after-mordant (see pp38–39). Add roughly one jar of the iron solution to a dye bath of around 4–5 litres (1 gallon). A mineral-based mordant alone gives good reds, or use an iron mordant on its own for brownish red. Otherwise use the mordant that best suits the fibre you're dyeing.

Madder (*Rubia tinctorum*) is native to Asia and Europe. Its genus name *Rubia* comes from the Latin word *ruber*, meaning 'red'. Madder was used as a medicinal plant by ancient civilisations and throughout the Middle Ages, and is still farmed for Ayurveda and Chinese medicine – it's believed to help alleviate blood disorders, jaundice, inflammation, kidney stones and dysentery, and to stimulate menstruation.

Its use as a dye dates back to the ancient Egyptians, who buried King Tutankhamun with a cloth dyed red, and in ancient China it was first employed more than 2,000 years ago during the Zhou Dynasty. During the 18th century, the famous British army 'redcoats' were produced using madder dye baths. It was only in 1869 that madder fell out of popularity, after scientists managed to synthesise

making a dye bath
Dried root

Weigh the fibre after it has been washed, scoured and dried. For a deep red, use 50–100% of the weight of the fibre in dried root – for example, for 400g (3½oz) of fibre, use 200–400g (1¾–3½oz) of madder root. For pale red, use 20% of the weight of the fibre in root – for example, for 400g (14oz) of fibre, use 80g (3oz) of root.

Grind it in a pestle and mortar or coffee grinder. Put the ground root into a cheesecloth and tie with string, like a makeshift tea bag, and place it in the dye pot. Fill with enough water to allow the fibre to move freely. The cheesecloth stops any larger particles from escaping, which might create inconsistencies in the dye results.

Leave for 24 hours. Alternatively, apply heat and simmer for 1 hour. After this time, remove the madder and use the liquid as the dye bath.

Dye powder

Weigh the fibre after it has been washed, scoured and dried. Use the same ratios and quantities as the dried root, above.

See p47 for how to make the dye powder dye bath.

dye bath method

Madder is suitable for use with either the cold dyeing, hot dyeing or the all-in-one dyeing method. See pp52–53 and follow the additional guidelines below.

If you live in a soft water area you might have trouble reaching a good red. If so, try adding chalk powder (calcium carbonate) to the dye bath, to bring out the redder tones – add 1 tsp per 100g (3½oz) of fibre. Alternatively, use slightly lower temperatures with the hot dyeing method.

For the hot dye method, heat for 30 minutes to 1 hour. It's important to keep the temperature of the water below a simmer for reds – if it goes above a simmer it can create browns. Do not allow the water to boil. For the cold dye method, leave for 2 days for a good red, or 3–4 days for a deeper shade.

After you've dyed the fibre, you can use the dye bath a second or third time to dye another fibre a lighter shade. In fact, it's good to have lots of fibre on hand to make the most of the multiple shades a madder dye bath offers.

modifier

Use an acidic modifier to shift the colours toward yellow and orange. An alkaline modifier gives pinker or redder tones.

avocado

The avocado (*Persea americana*) is a tree fruit, a large berry with a single large seed. In ancient Mayan culture it was a fruit of mystical magic and fertility, associated with healing, love and beauty. It was believed to have such a powerful influence on female fertility that young virgins were banned from leaving the family home during harvest season. Due to the lasting impact of these old stories, it's said there was a campaign to change the cultural attitude towards the fruits during the 19th century in order to boost the avocado industry.

Avocados are full of beneficial vitamins, minerals and antioxidants, including vitamins C and E. There are many different kinds, all of which are native to the tropics. The tree most likely originated in Mexico, but is now grown in many tropical and Mediterranean climates around the world.

The two kinds that are commonly imported are the Hass avocado, which has thick, dark purplish brown skin and an oval shape, and the Fuerte avocado, which has a thinner, smoother skin with a brighter green colour.

Recycling avocado skins and pits, rather than tossing them straight into the compost or bin, is a wonderful way to get a second life out of them – you can always add them to the compost for their remaining nutrients after using them as a dye material.

colour
The peel of the avocado offers a pale dusty blush, while the pit offers a slightly deeper pink tone.

source
Avocados can be difficult to grow as they prefer tropical climates and take at least 3–4 years to bear fruit. But luckily they're readily available in supermarkets. The peel and pits of all kinds of avocado can be used for their colour-giving properties. Collect them slowly over time as you use the fruit. You'll need to dry them or store them in a bag in the freezer until you are ready to use them. Alternatively, keep them submerged in water in a lidded bucket until you have collected enough for your dye bath.

type of dye / mordant *Substantive dye*
Because of its natural tannin content, avocado doesn't need to be paired with a mordant, but using one can deepen colours and strengthen the colourfastness of the dye. Use the mordant that best suits the fibre you're dyeing.

making a dye bath
Weigh the fibre after it has been washed, scoured and dried. For a deep pink, use 200% of the weight of the fibre in peel and/or pit – for example, for 400g (14oz) of fibre, use 800g (28oz) of avocado.

Wash the peel and/or whole pits (don't crush or cut the pits). Place them in a dye pot, cover with enough warm water to allow the fibre to move freely. Bring to the boil and boil for 30 minutes to 1 hour.

Strain with a fine sieve or muslin and use the liquid as the dye bath.

dye bath method
Suitable with either the cold dyeing or hot dyeing method. See pp52–53.

modifier
Acidic modifiers may cause a subtle shift to orangey tones, while an alkaline modifier can take the colour towards brown. An iron modifier can even shift hues to black.

dock

Dock is of the same genus (*Rumex*) as sorrel and the same family as rhubarb. There are many species of *Rumex*, and many of them can be used for dyeing.

Dock was originally found in the northern hemisphere, but has now been introduced all over the world. Although regarded as a weed, it is known for its ability to soothe stings. It is found in waste ground, near hedgerows, and on cultivated acid and calcareous soils. It grows to about 1m (1yd) tall and has leathery leaves that can be red or green.

Interestingly, dock has the chemical ability to transmute metallic iron into biological iron. So if you want to use a natural iron mordant in your work, you could place iron objects in the soil next to dock roots.

colour

The time of harvest will impact the dye results. I've used September-harvested red dock to get reddish-brown colours. Leaves harvested at other times (or from other species of dock) may yield shades of olive green, orange, brown or yellow.

source

Dock is regarded as an invasive species, so you will be doing your local farmer or gardener a favour by offering to remove it! But always ask the landowner first.

It's best to use the root, and winter is the best time to harvest. To spot the plant after it has died back, look for its long, tall stalk of flowers or seeds, which tower above it. The ground should be easier to dig into to remove the roots after rainfall. Mature plants give the strongest colours – you'll be surprised by how much colour comes out of a small amount of chopped dock root. You can also use the seeds for dyeing, or reserve them for bundle-dyeing projects.

type of dye/mordant *Substantive dye*

Dock does not need a mordant to fix its colour to animal fibres, but you will need one for plant fibres, otherwise the colour will be very pale. Dock naturally contains biological iron, which saddens the dye colour results, so for brighter colours use a mineral-based alum and cream of tartar mordant (see p31). Rich and deep colours can be achieved with a plant-based mordant, such as rhubarb leaf or oak gall.

making a dye bath
Fresh dock root

Weigh the fibre after it has been washed, scoured and dried. For a dark shade, use 300% of the weight of the fibre in dock root – for example, for 400g (14oz) of fibre, use 1.2kg (42oz) of dock root.

Scrub the roots well to remove any mud. Chop them up into tiny chunks, so that you have the maximum amount of surface area from which the dye can escape into the dye bath. Put the chunks in the dye pot and cover with enough warm water to allow the fabric to move freely.

Boil for at least 2 hours. Boiling the roots produces a strong, earthy aroma that can be unpleasant to some, so work in a well-ventilated area.

After boiling, leave to soak overnight. The next day, boil again for 1 hour. Leave to cool.

Strain through a fine sieve or muslin and use the liquid as the dye bath.

dye bath method

Suitable with either the cold dyeing, hot dyeing or all-in-one dyeing method. See pp52–53.

modifier

Depending on the species of dock that you use. PH modifiers will extend the range of colours only very subtly. An iron modifier can take colours into much darker tones, ranging from dark brown to grey and black.

onion

Onion (*Allium cepa*) is an allium, from the family Liliaceae. It is found on every continent and may have been growing wild everywhere since pre-civilisation. The ancient Egyptians believed the onion bestowed strength and that its concentric spherical rings symbolised eternity. In Alexandria, the royal army apparently ate onions to improve vitality, while the Romans gained strength and courage from these little golden orbs. Old folk recipes praise onion juice droplets as a cure for earache, a piece of raw onion on the forehead to help soothe migraines, and onion in a compress wrapped in cheesecloth on the chest to clear up coughs. It's said that in some rural places, onions were strung up in houses as protective magical amulets against sickness.

Brown and red onions are a classic home-dyer's choice – there's always a plentiful supply, and the colour they give is surprisingly rich, making them a favourite when you want an impressive result with little effort.

colour
Brown skins make beautiful yellow tones when kept below a boil, while boiling them provides rich burnt orange and rust-coloured dyes (this is what I've used for the fabrics in the image, left). Red skins offer slightly plummier tones. When used together, they create a vibrant, multi-dimensional hue.

source
Onions are easy to grow from sets and take 3–4 months to be ready to harvest. Store up supplies of onion skins from your own cooking – or if you need more, ask a local greengrocer for the waste from the bottom of their boxes, or get a café or food producer to put aside a bag for you. Apparently, over 500,000 tonnes of onion waste is thrown away every year in Europe. Imagine how much dye we could be making with all of that!

Store dry onion skins in paper bags, cardboard boxes or similar. Just make sure you're only keeping the dry skins, not any of the fleshy bits, and that they are fully dried out before going into storage, otherwise things can get smelly.

type of dye/mordant *Substantive dye*
Onion doesn't need to be paired with a mordant, but using one deepens colours and strengthens the colourfastness of the dye. You should use the mordant that best suits the fibre you're dyeing.

making a dye bath
Weigh the fibre after it has been washed, scoured and dried. For a deep shade, use 50% of the weight of the fibre in skin – for example, for 400g (14oz) of fibre, use 200g (7oz) of onion.

Onion skins are super-easy and quick to dye with. No need to chop them, simply put them in the dye pot and pour in enough water to allow the fibre to move freely.

Bring to a simmer, and simmer for 30 minutes. You'll see the colour of the water changing and deepening quite quickly.

Strain out the onion skins and use the liquid as the dye bath.

dye bath method
Suitable with the hot dyeing method. See pp52–53 and follow the additional guidelines below.

For the hot dye, simmer for about 30 minutes, or until you have the desired shade.

You can use the dye bath a second time to get paler shades.

modifier
An acidic modifier shifts colours towards orangey yellow. An alkaline modifier moves colours towards green.

eucalyptus

Eucalyptus is named for its cup-like buds, after the Greek word *eucalyptos*, meaning 'well covered'. Australian Aboriginal people have used eucalyptus from time immemorial to treat fevers and all kinds of ailments. The essential oil is generally distilled from the leaves and has medicinal and antibacterial properties. It is one of the oils most commonly used in aromatherapy, and it's often used by herbalists to help loosen congestion and ease coughs: it's inhaled over steam baths, or used topically to relieve muscle and joint pains. For more spiritual uses, eucalyptus makes a lovely smudge stick for purifying spaces in preparation for sacred rituals and ceremonies. Alternatively, it's great for clearing the air after an argument!

You could try hanging an unused branch of eucalyptus over your shower for a refreshing bathing ritual experience. I love having it around to decorate gifts, hang on the wall or put into flower arrangements and bouquets, offering interactive olfactory sensations to passers-by.

There are over 400 species, but *Eucalyptus globulus* is the most commonly found – it is often introduced to new places, as it does so well in poor soil conditions. It also grows rapidly – it can be harvested in 14–16 years (compared to the usual 60 years of other trees), making it an appealing option for renewable timber. If you want to plant your own, it is worth considering that it is an invasive species and can damage plant diversity.

colour
Eucalyptus dye colours range from deep orange to reddish-brown from the leaves, and lighter hues of pinky-beige from the bark. I've used leaves to dye the fabrics in the image on the right.

source
You can harvest the leaves at any time of the year, and they are best collected from the ground after they have fallen from the branches. They can even be used after the leaf colour has faded to brown, as the dye pigment is still in the leaf.

type of dye/mordant *Substantive dye*
The rich tannin content of the plant gives substantive qualities, meaning mordants aren't essential, but they can be used to extend the life of colours and to obtain a wider range of shades. Use the mordant that best suits the fibre you're dyeing.

making a dye bath
Weigh the fibre after it has been washed, scoured and dried. For a good deep shade, use 100% of the weight of the fibre in leaves or bark – for example, for 400g (14oz) of fibre, use 400g (14oz) of eucalyptus. For a dye bath using bark, follow the instructions on p49.

For a dye bath using leaves, chop the leaves up very small so they look shredded – the smaller you can chop them the better, as this creates a larger surface area for the colour to escape into the water.

Place the finely chopped leaves into a dye pot and just cover with boiling water. Wait a few moments before topping up with enough warm water to allow your fibre to move freely. Simmer for 2–3 hours. Then leave to sit overnight. Strain through a fine sieve or muslin and use the liquid as a dye bath.

dye bath method
Suitable with the hot dyeing or the all-in-one method. See pp52–53 and follow the additional guidelines below.

For hot dyeing, bring to a boil for 2–3 hours (keep at a simmer for an animal fibre), before leaving overnight.

The discarded leaves can be used again to create a second dye bath.

modifier
An acidic modifier gives pinky shades, while an alkaline modifier moves colours toward muddier browns.

bracken

Bracken (*Pteridium aquilinum*) is a type of deciduous fern – it's one of the oldest ferns known, with fossils dating back over 55 million years. It was once believed to bring eternal youth and invisibility to the possessor, as mentioned in Shakespeare's *Henry IV*: 'We have the receipt of Fern seed – we walk invisible.'

The young shoots, known as 'fiddleheads', are eaten in many Asian cultures – for example, in Korea they are mixed into the traditional dish *bibimbap*. Others use the root, which can be ground down to give a starchy flour for making bread or jellies. Ancient civilisations used both the fronds and stems in medicinal drinks, and they are still used to make a traditional wild beer in various countries, including Russia and Norway.

Do note, however, that there are noxious compounds in both fronds and roots, and they should not be eaten. The spores on the underside of the leaf are considered carcinogenic if regularly breathed in, but do not pose a high risk if you're casually visiting an area planted with bracken.

Easily recognised by its large triangular fronds, which grow up to 2m (8ft) high, bracken is commonly found on moorland across most continents. It's seen by some as an invasive plant as it colonises land quickly, driving out other species of moorland plant, while others appreciate the canopy it offers to other plant life where woodland no longer exists. For those with access to bracken-laden land, it's worth knowing its high potash content means it can be used as a valuable green manure.

colour

Bracken gives a range of yellow-green to olive green and greeny-brown shades. The colours vary from place to place and depending on the time of year you harvest – I've had a random mixture of browns, yellow-browns, olive greens and coppery-greens from different batches.

source

Bracken fronds can be harvested throughout the growing season, before they die back in autumn/winter. Avoid harvesting in late summer when spores are released.

Bracken fronds are tough and can be sharp against the skin, so always wear gloves when harvesting them, and use a pair of scissors or secateurs to chop them at the nodules where the leaves join the stem.

Always ask the landowner before harvesting, and look out for local farmers cutting back the bracken at certain times of year – a great opportunity to recycle unwanted plant material.

type of dye / mordant *Adjective dye*

It's best to use a mordant with bracken to get deeper hues and longer-lasting results. Use the mordant that best suits the fibre you're dyeing.

making a dye bath

Weigh the fibre after it has been washed, scoured and dried. For a deep shade, use 100% of the weight of the fibre in fresh, feathery fronds – for example, for 400g (14oz) of fibre, use 400g (14oz) of bracken.

See p48 for how to make a dye bath using leaves.

dye bath method

Suitable with the hot dyeing method. See pp52–53.

modifier

An acidic modifier produces lighter shades, while an alkaline modifier gives rich and deep red brick tones.

nettle

Nettle (*Urtica dioica*) is a much undervalued wild perennial with numerous useful qualities, from its tough fibre – great for making rope – to its high nutritional value.

It's thought nettles were once used to mark the dwelling places of fairies and other magical creatures, and people would harness its protective energy to dispel dark magic – or deter naughty spirits from causing mischief – by sprinkling its leaves about their homes or carrying dried leaf on their bodies in a pouch.

Herbalists have traditionally used nettles to tackle hayfever, heart conditions, high blood pressure, arthritis, kidney and bladder problems and slow circulation, as well as to help balance blood sugar and cortisol levels.

Nettles are higher in iron and vitamin C than many other more obvious sources, so make a great addition to your diet to boost mineral uptake. I like to gather extra nettles to make into a soup or pesto, especially at the beginning of the growing season. You can try collecting and drying them, and keeping a pot of the dried seeds to sprinkle on your food for added minerals and vitamins.

colour
The colours that nettles offer vary from hues of yellowish green if harvested in early spring, to olive green if harvested in late summer (the colour often becomes darker later in the year). The soil they grow in, the weather and the climate all play a role in the colour outcome. You can also use the root to make a bright yellow dye.

source
When harvesting the plant use gloves to protect your hands from being stung. Use normal household scissors to snip off the first two tiers of leaves, or the top 15cm (6in) of the plant – I aim to cut at the nodes, which is where the leaves join the stem. If you cut the stem at this point, you will encourage a new growth of leaves.

I use a basket to collect the leaves, then give it a bit of a shake and leave it on the ground for an hour before processing so that any tiny stowaway bugs and insects have a chance to escape!

type of dye / mordant *Adjective dye*
Use the mordant that best suits the fibre you're dyeing.

making a dye bath
Weigh the fibre after it has been washed, scoured and dried. You'll need 200% of the weight of the fibre in fresh leaves – for example, for 400g (14oz) of fibre, use 800g (24oz) of nettle.

See p48 for how to make a dye bath using leaves.

Once you have made and strained the dye, you can use any leftover plant material as a green manure or compost to enrich the soil in your garden. Or make a liquid feed for garden plants by simply soaking it in water for 1–3 weeks then straining it to get a fertiliser liquid.

dye bath method
Suitable with the hot dyeing method. See pp52–53.

modifier
Use iron as an alkaline modifier to get a deep, earthy green, or try an acidic modifier for warmer colours.

chlorophyllin

The name chlorophyllin comes from the ancient Greek *chloros* meaning 'green', and *phyllon*, which means 'leaf'. Chlorophyll is responsible for the alchemical process of photosynthesis, in which light from the sun is converted into biological energy inside plant cells.

Chlorophyllin is a green pigment, which is extracted from plants such as nettle, alfalfa and mint, and has long been used as an alternative topical medicine for wounds and burns, in natural beauty products as a deodorant, and for skin protection.

It's relatively new as a dye for textiles and crafts, but has been readily adopted by the natural home-dyeing community as green has historically been the hardest colour to achieve. Previously, dyers would overdye indigo (blue) with weld (yellow), which resulted in an earthy green, rather than the vivid and vibrant shade of chlorophyllin.

colour
Chlorophyllin produces a range of greens, from pale tones to deep forest and emerald sea.

source
You can buy chlorophyllin online as extract powder.

type of dye / mordant *Adjective dye*
Use with a mordant to lengthen the life of the colours. Use the mordant that best suits the fibre you're dyeing.

making a dye bath
Weigh the fibre after it has been washed, scoured and dried. For a good green, use 5% of the weight of the fibre in extract powder – for example, for 400g (14oz) of fibre, use 20g (½oz) of chlorophyllin.

See p47 for how to make an extract powder dye bath.

dye bath method
Suitable with the hot dyeing method.

See pp52–53 and follow the additional guidelines below.

For deeper colours, it's best to layer the colour (see p53). Simply mordant the fibre again after dyeing and return to the dye bath. This is better than adding more extract powder to the first dye bath.

modifier
Chlorophyllin is very pH-stable and therefore doesn't change colour dramatically when acidic or alkaline modifiers are applied.

weld

Rich levels of luteolin are what give weld its bright yellow dye colour. This was eventually synthesised by scientists at the end of the 20th century, although weld had already fallen out of popular use following the invention of coal tar-derived dyes in the late 19th to early 20th century.

The plant is a yellow-flowering biennial, growing up to 1.5m (5ft) tall. The flowers give off an incredible sweet aphrodisiac scent, and are loved by bees, butterflies and insects. They are dried for use in potpourri and the fragrant oil is used in perfume, as well as an oil for lighting.

colour

Weld gives a brilliant bright yellow, which is often used for overdyeing indigo-dyed fibres to create beautiful emerald, leaf green and teal – as well as Lincoln green, the famous colour of Robin Hood's clothing, and another medieval hue, Saxon green. It can also be used to overdye madder-dyed fibre to create oranges.

The quality of the local water you are using will dictate the outcome of the dye colour to some extent, as will the type of soil the plant has grown in.

Weld is soluble in hot water and alcohol, so it's great for use as a drawing ink as well as a dye (see p129).

source

All parts of the plant are used, especially the tops, which flower from June to August. However, most of the dye is found within the seed, which is harvested as the flowers start to disappear at the end of summer.

The best colour comes from plants with yellow or greenish flowers and an abundance of foliage. When handling the plant wear gloves to avoid potential irritation to sensitive skin. Weld can be used in either fresh or dried form. You can source dried weld online.

type of dye/mordant *Adjective dye*

Yellow tends to be the dye colour that fades most quickly, but weld has proved to have better colourfastness than other sources of yellow. It's still best used with a mordant to lengthen the life of the colour. Use the mordant that best suits the fibre you're dyeing.

Weld (*Reseda luteola*) is a native plant of Europe and Asia, but has been naturalised around the world. The name *reseda* means healer or restorer – it literally translates to 'gives comfort' in Latin. The Romans used it medicinally for its narcotic value, as a sedative and poultice, and to treat bites, stings and small wounds.

Its yellow dye is one of the oldest known in the world, along with madder and indigo – it was used by the ancient Greeks and the Romans, who are believed to have dyed the robes of their Vestal Virgins with it. It was used as an ink to illuminate medieval manuscripts and by Vermeer in his painting *Girl with a Pearl Earring*.

making a dye bath
Dried

Weigh the fibre after it has been washed, scoured and dried. Use 50% of the weight of the fibre in dried weld – for example, for 400g (14oz) of fibre, use 200g (7oz) of weld. Break up the weld and leave it to soak overnight in warm water.

The next day, chop up the weld and cover with enough water to allow the fibre to move freely. Bring it up to a simmer, and then simmer for 1 hour. Be careful not to let the liquid boil, as this will mute the weld colour from bright to murky.

Stir gently every now and then to encourage extraction from all parts of the plant material. After this, strain through a fine sieve or muslin and use the liquid as the dye bath.

Fresh

Weigh the fibre after it has been washed, scoured and dried. You'll need 50% of the weight of the fibre in fresh weld – for example, for 400g (14oz) of fibre, use 200g (7oz) of weld. Chop the leaves, flowers and stalks and add to the dye pot with enough water to allow the fibre to move freely.

Bring it to a simmer, put the lid on the pot, and then simmer for 30 minutes. Be careful not to let the liquid boil, as this will mute the colour from bright to murky.

Strain and use the liquid as the dye bath.

dye bath method

Suitable with the hot dyeing method. See pp52–53 and follow the additional guidelines below.

Simmering for 30 minutes to 1 hour gives yellow, but boiling for the same time gives a mustard hue.

If you find it difficult to achieve a bright, light yellow, try adding a small amount of chalk powder (calcium carbonate) to the dye bath. Keep the fibre in the dye bath, add about 1 tsp per 100g (3½oz) of fibre. Stir, then simmer for 1 hour more.

You may also find that a slightly longer dyeing time improves the colour.

As weld is slightly soluble in hot water, dyed items should always be washed in cold water only.

modifier

Both acidic and alkaline modifiers give clearer and brighter yellows. An iron solution used as a modifier moves the colour toward a moss or murky green.

logwood

Logwood (*Haematoxylum campechianum*) is native to Mexico and Central America, especially the Gulf of Campeche, but in 1715 it was introduced to Jamaica and various other Caribbean islands and naturalised.

You can identify this small flowering tree by its crooked, spiny branches, dark and roughly textured bark, small yellow flowers and the interesting leaf formation of heart-shaped pairs.

The part used by dyers is the inner heartwood of the tree, which is a rich red colour – hence its scientific name, which comes from the Greek *haima*, meaning blood, and *xylon* meaning wood. The heartwood was exported to Europe from the 17th to the 19th centuries for use as a dye material, although it's now less valuable to commercial exporters. However, it is still widely exploited for its haematoxylin, which scientists use to stain plant and animal cells for observation.

colour
Logwood offers lovely soft shades of violet, deeper purples and bluey-black. Shades of purple vary a lot, depending on the type of fibre, water and mordant, and purple can only be achieved when heat is applied, otherwise it yields black.

source
Many logwood exports are sourced from an unsustainable logging industry, so if you choose to work with logwood it's important that you buy the material from certified organic, fairtrade and sustainable sources.

You can use either logwood extract powder, or wood chips, both of which are available online.

type of dye / mordant *Substantive dye*
It's best to use a mordant with this dye, as it's not very colourfast. An iron solution mordant is more helpful for extending the life of the colour and for achieving darker shades of blue and black.

making a dye bath
Logwood extract powder is potent and you'll only need a very minimal amount to dye with. Weigh the fibre after it has been washed, scoured and dried. You'll need 2% of the weight of the fibre in extract powder – for example, for 400g (14oz) of fibre, use 8g (⅓oz) of logwood. Or for dried chips, use 30% of the weight of the fibre.

You can use less for paler tones, but if you want a darker colour, it's best to layer dye the fibre to build up the colour (see p53).

See p47 for how to make an extract powder or wood chip dye bath.

dye bath method
Suitable with the hot dyeing method. See pp52–53 and follow the additional guidelines below.

Bring the dye bath to a simmer for 45 minutes to 1 hour, then leave it to soak overnight.

You can dry any leftover plant material to keep for future use.

Do note that logwood is particularly pH-sensitive, so it's worth considering its suitability for different projects. It may not be the best option for clothing, as small splashes of salad dressing can change your look quite quickly!

modifier
Because logwood is so pH-sensitive, it turns from light purple to brown with an acidic modifier, and moves toward a deep purple with an alkaline modifier. Iron gives good bluey-blacks.

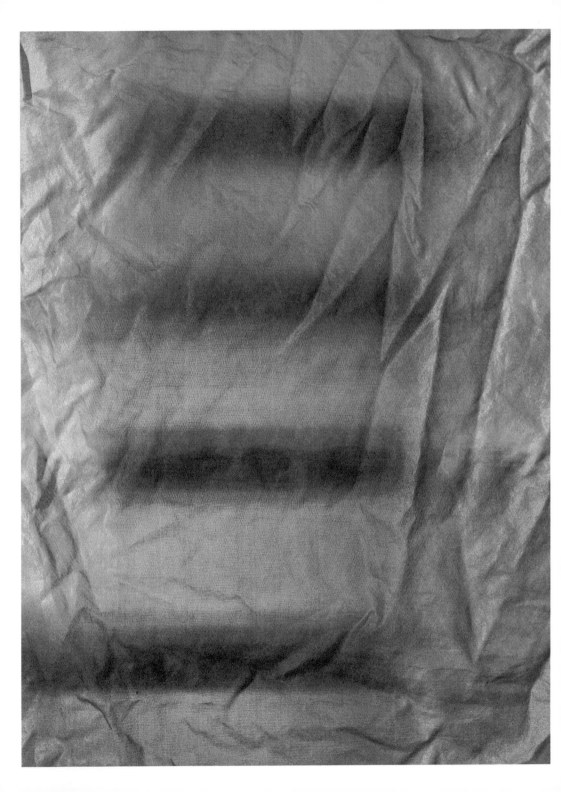

cutch

The acacia is a long-revered tree with a spirit that calls for renewal, fortitude and purity. In some traditional rituals its evergreen leaves are said to represent immortality. Its sacred wood is used to build temples throughout Asia and some historians suggest it may have been the Tree of Life and the Burning Bush of the Bible. The plant is burned in sacred rituals in the Far East and to clear space of malevolent energies in Tibet. With this in mind, you may enjoy working with this dye to transform your clothing and textiles into empowering and supportive amulets.

Cutch has been used as a medicine to purify blood and rejuvenate skin for centuries. In Ayurvedic medicine, it is used for its astringent qualities, while in modern-day France and Italy it is an ingredient in breath-freshening pastilles. It is also used in South Asian cooking to make breath-freshening *paan masala* and *gutka*, a form of chewing tobacco.

Cutch comes from the heartwood of the cutch tree (*Acacia catechu*), which is common to most of India, Burma, Indonesia and Peru. The name describes the colour of the earth in the region of the same name in Gujarat, India – a khaki given by the dye, which has been used to colour army uniforms. The Indian word translates to 'earth' or 'soil'. To extract the dye the heartwood of the tree is soaked in hot water until the water becomes thick. It is then cooled and pressed into blocks. Once fully dried, these are ground into a powder.

Cutch contains the natural dye chemical catechu along with tannic acid, which acts as both a dye and a mordant. Its high tannin content means it is also used in leather tanning. From the early 19th century, it was the preferred product for tanning animal hides as it was less expensive than other materials such as oak tannin.

colour
Earthy cinnamon shades of beige to light chestnut brown. Longer dye times bring out pink shades.

source
You can buy cutch online as an extract powder.

type of dye / mordant *Substantive dye*
Cutch is naturally high in tannins/tannic acid, so an additional mordant is not necessary. However, alum brightens colours, creating pinker/peachier/more yellow/ orange shades. An oak gall tannin mordant gives a different dye colour, with a more greyish/beige tone to it. Iron will sadden to grey-browns.

making a dye bath
Weigh the fibre after it has been washed, scoured and dried. Use 15% of the weight of the fibre to dye a light cinnamon – for example, for 400g (14oz) of fibre, use 60g (2¼oz) of cutch extract – 20% of the weight of the fibre for a light chestnut brown, and 30% for a medium chestnut brown.

Put the required amount of powder in a bowl and add a few drops of boiling water to make a paste. As it is a heartwood material, it is a little resinous and takes some extra work to smooth out lumps and dissolve properly into a solution. Once smooth, add a few more teaspoonfuls of boiling water to make an ink.

To make a dye, add enough hot water so that your fibres have space to move around freely. Heat the fibres for 30 minutes to 1 hour until the desired depth of colour is acquired. Leave to saturate overnight for deeper shades. Remove and wash, rinse and air dry.

There will be plenty of dye still available after your first batch to colour a few extra items lighter shades.

dye bath method
Use a hot dye bath. See pp52–53.

Colours can appear more reddish on protein/animal fibres, and more brown on cellulose/plant fibres.

modifier
Cutch is very pH stable. An alkaline modifier such as soda ash shifts colours to pink/red shades, or mix with other natural dyes to expand a colour range of browns. Over-dye with indigo for a grey-green.

common hawthorne

Common hawthorne (*Crataegus monogyna*) is one of the ancient native trees of the British Isles and found commonly across Europe and North America as a hedgerow plant. Blossoming in May – hence its other name of maythorn – it is considered a fairy tree and when found alongside ash and oak a place of fairy lore. Its thorns partly explain why the tree is considered protective and was gathered and brought into the home as a protective amulet each year. The five-petal pentagram shape of the flowers is also said to be magical.

This tree is closely linked to May Day or Beltane, the festival of fertility, in Britain. The flowers (mayflowers) would have been in bloom on May Day – until a revision of the calendar in 1752 brought May 1 forward by 13 days and took the holiday out of sync with the season. The fragrance of the flowers was thought to transport you to another state of being more connected to the heart and fertility.

The beauty of this dye not only lies in the warm colours it yields but also in its parent plant's heart-benefiting actions. Hawthorne berries are one of the most important natural heart and circulatory tonics in traditional herbal medicine. They are believed to normalise both high and low blood pressure, improve overall heart function and support weak or damaged hearts both physically and emotionally, as well as benefiting circulation, stress and heart tension, nervous heart problems, irregular heartbeats and other heart ailments.

colour
Hawthorne creates beautiful dusty rose pinks, from light to darker shades on plant fibres and more orangey colours on animal fibres.

source
Commonly found in hedgerows throughout Europe and North America. Always harvest in a way that is kind to the tree or plant, and don't over-harvest. The whole twiggy branch can be used, including leaves, flowers and berries.

type of dye/mordant *Substantive dye*
Mordant with alum for brighter and deeper colours. The tannin in the branches and leaves helps fix the colour and so an additional mordant is not necessary but helps improve fastness.

making a dye bath
Chop the branches, leaves and berries into small chunks and cover with water. Use 500% of the weight of the fibre – for example, for 400g (14oz) of fibre, use 2kg (70oz) of hawthorne branches, leaves and berries. If you can leave them to soak for a day or two, this will help soften the matter and allow it to release its colour more easily. Boil for 2–3 hours. If you have more time, you can leave overnight and then boil again for an hour or two the next day to release maximum colour. Allow to cool gently before removing the plant matter from the dye water with a sieve and cheesecloth.

dye bath method
Suitable with the hot dyeing method. See pp52–53 and follow the additional guidelines below.

Animal fibres can be gently simmered for 1 hour while plant fibres can be boiled for longer until the desired depth of colour is reached. You can also leave your fibre in the dye bath overnight to cool and obtain deeper saturation.

modifier
Use an alkaline modifier to shift colours into deeper darker shades.

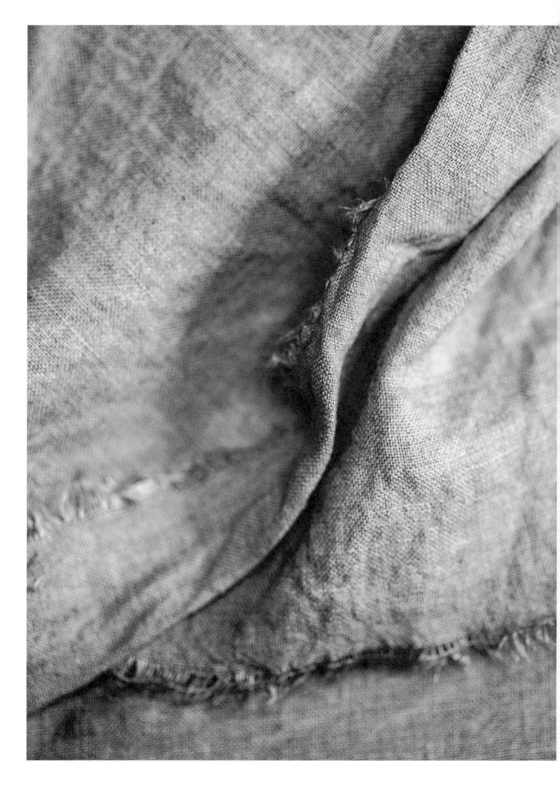

marigold

Marigold flowers shine and glow with a heart-expanding and joyous radiance. They restore the body's physical boundaries, while illuminating one's sense of self. Where other herbs offer to move stagnation, marigold shines a bright light guiding us back to our natural state of vitality.

The ancient Romans and Greeks used marigold in many rituals and ceremonies, sometimes wearing the flowers in crowns or garlands. One of its nicknames is 'Mary's Gold', which refers to the flowers' use in early Catholic events. The flowers are sacred in India and have been used to decorate the statues of Hindu deities since early times. In Mexico they are used to illuminate pathways to guide spirits home during the Day of the Dead.

Marigold has traditionally been used as both a culinary and medicinal herb. Its edible petals can beautify salads while its dried form can colour cooked foods and cosmetics. Medicinally, its antioxidant and anti-microbial qualities help heal wounds. The flowers are a rich source of lutein, a carotenoid pigment, which is known to improve eye health. Marigold ointments are used to soothe skin irritations such as eczema and psoriasis, cooling inflamed sensations, while marigold teas calm fragmented nerves.

In permaculture gardening marigold is not only a beautiful decorative plant, but also a useful companion plant that improves the wellness of neighbouring species. Gardeners often plant it around vegetable patches to create protective borders that keep away pests and bugs.

colour
Strong, vibrant yellows, green-yellows and oranges depending on the dye concentration and mordant.

source
Organic marigold dye mix extract powder is available from my website, along with whole dried marigold flowers grown organically in the British Isles. Use dye extract powder for immersion dyeing and whole flowers for bundle dyeing and eco printing.

type of dye/mordant *Adjective dye*
Marigold has good fastness to both sunlight and to rubbing and washing. Some studies have even shown that it has better fastness to washing, perspiration and rubbing than some synthetically dyed fabrics. An alum mordant brightens yellows on animal fibres and orangey yellows on plant fibres. Adding 3% iron powder to the pot produces olive greens.

making a dye bath
Whole dried flowers
Weigh the fibre after it has been washed, scoured and dried. Use 20% of the weight of the fibre for medium depth of shade – for example, for 400g (14oz) of fibre, use 80g (2¾oz) of whole dried flowers.

Add to a pot, cover with water, simmer for half an hour to extract the dye, then strain with a sieve and cheesecloth. Add the fibres and simmer gently on a low heat until the desired shade is achieved.

Extract powder
Weigh the fibre after it has been washed, scoured and dried. Use 10% of the weight of fibre to dye a light yellow – for example, for 400g (14oz) of fibre, use 40g (1½oz) of marigold extract powder. For a medium yellow, use 20% of the weight of the fibre and for a deep yellow, use 30%.

Put the required amount of powder in a bowl and add a few drops of water to make a paste. Smooth out any lumps before adding a few teaspoonfuls of water to make an ink.

To make a dye, add enough water so your fibres have space to move around freely. Bring to a simmer and keep at 82°C (180°F) for 30 minutes. Strain using a sieve and cheesecloth. Add pre-wetted fibres and simmer for 1 hour or until the desired depth of colour is achieved.

dye bath method
Use the hot dyeing method. See pp52–53.

modifiers
Marigold is pH sensitive. A tiny measure of an alkaline modifier such as soda ash shifts yellows to more orangey shades. Over-dyeing with indigo creates warm leaf greens.

dyer's coreopsis

Dyer's coreopsis (*Coreopsis tinctoria*) is a beautiful dye flower from the prairies of North America, where it has been used for ceremonial dyeing, fertility rituals and protection against the damages of lightning. The flowers often appear in displays of red and yellow colourings that easily hybridise and create new variations when grown together.

This sacred plant has been woven into ritualistic practices across many different Native American tribes. The Cherokee, Zuni and Apache made a ceremonial red dye from it, while the Navajo used it to create a ceremonial balm and as a cold infusion to treat 'lightning infection' – inflammation caused by material given off by lightning. Native Americans also made a tea from the roots to treat diarrhoea and brewed the dried tops of the plant to strengthen the blood. It was also thought to have magical properties that helped women conceive female children.

In traditional Chinese medicine, dyer's coreopsis is used to help with high blood pressure, insomnia, and inflammation.

You can use it to make a wonderfully rich dye bath for immersion dyeing and to add beautiful splashes of deep orange as part of a bundle-dye process.

colour
Yellows, orange, reddish orange, copper, rust, beige and brown. You get the best colours on animal fibres, with results on plant fibres less interesting.

source
Dyer's coreopsis is found across North America and other temperate regions and grows well in British dye gardens, attracting beneficial insects and pollinators such as bees and butterflies. Use the flower heads for dyeing purposes (deadheaded flowers are fine too).

type of dye/mordant *Adjective dye*
Dyer's coreopsis has good fastness, which is improved with a mordant such as alum for brighter, deeper shades. Alum gives best results on protein fibres, and is not recommended for dyeing cellulose fibres. Adding iron shifts the colour towards green.

making a dye bath
Cover the flowers with water, soak overnight, and gently simmer on a low heat for 30 mins to 1 hour to release their colour. Use 50% of the weight of fibre in whole dyer's coreopsis flowers – for example, for 400g (14oz) of fibre, use 200g (7oz) of flowers. Strain with a sieve and cheesecloth.

dye bath method
Suitable with the hot dyeing method. See pp52–53 and follow the additional guidelines below.

Gently heat your fibre at just below simmering point for 30–60 minutes. A more reddish orange colour can appear first with a secondary exhaust colour of yellow possible later as the plant tends to contain two dye colours.

modifier
Sensitive to changes in pH level. A weak acidic modifier shifts colours towards yellow and an alkaline modifier can move oranges into reds.

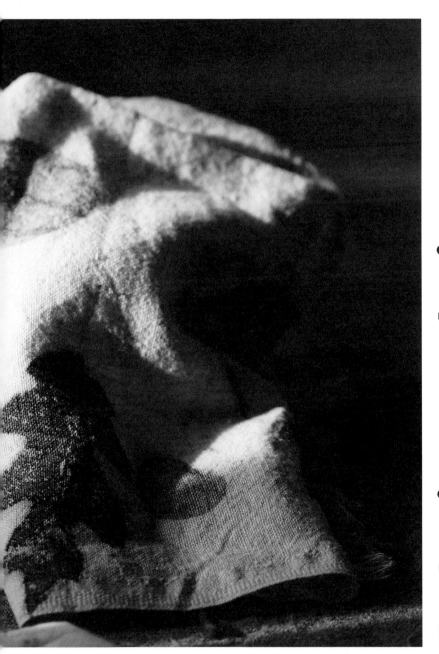

5 dyeing techniques

bundle dyeing

Bundle dyeing, also known as eco-printing, is a contemporary process developed by Australian textile artist India Flint. As a child she enjoyed the traditions of her Latvian heritage, which included dyeing Easter eggs with onion skins and imprinting them with leaves and herbs. As an adult, she applied the same concept to fabric, and found that the plant dyes gave direct impressions, just as they did on the eggs.

This wonderfully alchemical process uses the botanical dyes from fresh flowers, leaves and other plant material to create herbal-infused prints. The print is formed when the plant transfers its colour onto the fabric (or paper). The need for dye extraction or a dye bath is entirely skipped out, making this a particularly quick technique.

Mesmerising repeat patterns can be made using different folding, rolling and binding styles, offering brilliantly unique prints. And because the results are so unpredictable, this is a great opportunity to be playful and experimental, and for using mindfulness and intuitive herbalism to guide you in your creative journey. Notice how the plants impact your mood, spirit and physical sensations, and the emotions and memories they stir up. If you slow down and pay attention, it can be interesting to see what comes through.

Many flowers give bright, exciting hues to begin with, but tend to fade after they have dried, are washed or age a little. You will find that some are more colourfast than others, and I invite you to go out and explore your local bio-region to discover your own colour palette and learn which plants are your favourites to use for their different colours, shapes, fastness or herbal characteristics.

you will need
Fabric (washed, scoured and mordanted)
Clear or light-coloured vinegar in a mister bottle
Plant material (fresh petals, leaves, stems, berries and such like)
Dye powder or extract powder (optional)
Dried flowers (optional)
String or rubber bands
Steaming equipment (for hot dyeing)
Tongs
Glass jar with lid or plastic bag (for cold dyeing)

plant material
A wide variety of fresh and dried flowers and plants can be used for this technique. I like to use rich, dark-coloured flowers, especially viola, delphinium, iris, pelargonium, petunia, black-purple hollyhock, dark red roses, cornflower, marigold, passion flower, heather, chrysanthemum and geranium. You can use other plant parts too, such as berries, leaves, roots and seeds and even some waste foods such as onion skins.

I enjoy building up seasonal layers of prints by foraging the things around me through the different parts of the year, and creating a story of the plants that have come and gone, leaving their impression behind on my cloth.

Most natural dye and extract powders work well when sprinkled lightly onto the surface too. Their intense colour tends to bleed and saturate well, so very little is required.

fabric
Silk (animal fibre) is ideal for this technique. It absorbs the plant colour and holds on to it very well. I recommend you start out by using an organic, soft, tightly woven silk, such as a habotai, satin or crêpe de chine, although any kind of tightly woven animal fibre should work well. You can use plant fibres, such as hemp or linen, too, but they will need a longer mordanting and dyeing process.

mordant
Silk doesn't need a mordant but it's worth considering one if you intend to use the fabric to make a garment you'll wear a lot, or if the fabric will be exposed to lots of sunlight.

Using a mineral-based mordant such as alum and cream of tartar (see p31) helps brighten the colours and extend their life. I also like to use rhubarb leaf mordant as it gives the finished piece beautiful muted tones that can be easier to wear if you're turning your printed fabric into a garment.

modifier
You could use a modifier such as iron water, which mutes the colours and gives the finished bundle-dye a melancholy, bluish tinge.

process

1. Make sure the fabric is washed and scoured, and mordanted. You can use it while it's still damp from the mordanting process. If the fabric is dry, pre-wet it (see p26) first, as this helps the colours to move through the fabric well.

2. Lay it out so that the whole piece of fabric is spread out before you on a table. If space is limited, you can work on one section of the fabric at a time.

3. Use a mister bottle to spray the fibre with vinegar until it is saturated. Vinegar has an acidic pH, which means that it helps to brighten colours. I use organic apple cider vinegar as it's local to me, though you can use any vinegar that's suitable for you. Just avoid the darker kinds, such as balsamic vinegar, as they aren't as effective at brightening the colours.

4. Scatter the plant materials across the cloth as you wish, perhaps breaking up petals and leaves or sometimes leaving them whole. I tend to be quite random about what I do, and really get into the process of making a mess with beautiful natural things! Some people like to make pretty arrangements and motifs with their leaves and flowers, but it never comes out quite as they might expect. It's always a surprise when you open the bundle later, and it's impossible to control the exact outcome. The best thing is to experiment. Try out a few different techniques for scattering and arranging the plant material.

5. It's nice to leave a little blank space between the materials instead of totally covering the surface; some space gives definition to the pattern. But do try to bring the plant material right up to the edges, so that you don't end up with an empty border around the sides. You can also sprinkle dye powder or extract powder onto the fabric.

6. Once you have scattered material across the piece, spray it again with vinegar. You can then start to bundle it up – there are a million ways you can try, but I like to use two different techniques for this.

Concertina fold

1. This method creates interesting symmetrical repeat patterns by folding the cloth like an accordion. To do this, concertina fold (as if you were making a fan with a sheet of paper) the piece of fabric back and forth until you have a narrow length of cloth.

2. Turn it vertically to face you, then concertina fold the narrow length of fabric until you have a small, square-ish bundle.

3. Alternatively, you can fold the fabric in half and in half again and again and again, until it can't be folded up any smaller. You can add more petals into each new fold if you wish, to create more layers of pattern, or you can leave it with just the initial layer. Give it a little spray with vinegar with each new fold.

4. Once you have made the bundle, use some string or rubber bands and secure it tightly. The idea is that the fibre and the plant material are as closely pressed together as possible, so that the dye can transfer from one to the other.

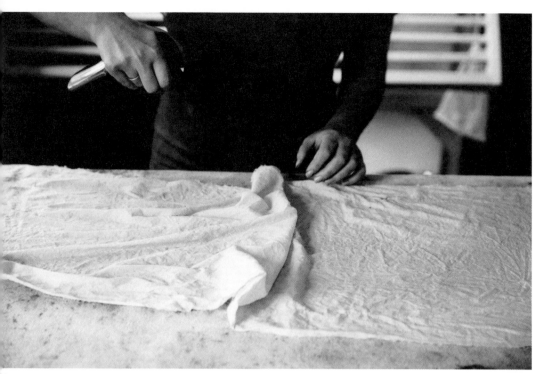

Spraying the fabric with vinegar; Scattering plant material

From top left: Concertina fold; Folding the fabric; Rolling method;
The final rolled and concertina-folded bundles

Rolling

1. This method gives a more linear repeat pattern. Starting at one end of the fabric, roll it into a sausage shape with the plant material inside. Do this as tightly as possible.

2. Once you've rolled it one way, turn it vertically to face you, and then roll it again, as tight as you can, to make a spiral shape. You may like to do a bit of both: some folding and then a bit of rolling. There are no rules! Only endless ways to try.

3. Once you have made the bundle, use some string or rubber bands and secure it tightly. You want the fibre and the plant material to be as closely pressed together as possible.

cold dyeing method

Simply put the bundle into a glass jar with a lid, or a plastic bag firmly tied closed, and leave for several weeks – at least 1 week, or until you can't bear to wait any longer! If mould starts to appear, this can be remedied by taking the bundle out of the jar or bag and putting it in the freezer, or steaming it for 30 minutes. Then put it back in the jar or bag and carry on with the process.

hot dyeing method

Steaming the bundle speeds up the dye process. See p42 for steaming tips. Steam for 1 hour, turning it over every 15 minutes. Then turn off the heat and leave it to cool.

compost dyeing method

I prefer to use a zero-energy approach for bundle dyeing. Wrap the fabric up in a protective cloth or bag. Dig a hole in a compost heap, then place the protected fabric in the hole and cover with more compost. The natural acids and heat mix with and morph the botanical colours into really interesting hues. Leave for a few weeks or months – simply come back to it when you remember, or when curiosity gets the better of you. If mould starts to appear, follow the remedy from the cold dyeing method, then return the bundle to the compost heap.

solar dyeing method

Another great low-energy technique for applying heat. Place your bundle into a lidded, sealed glass jar. Leave on a window sill for several weeks, where it can catch the sun's warming rays.

post-dyeing

1. Once you have completed the dye process, unwrap the bundle outdoors so you can shake off the plant materials.

2. Hang the fabric to air dry in a shady spot, out of direct sunlight. Once dry, remove any last pieces of plant material stuck to the fabric.

3. Use a steam iron and press cloth to steam press it.

4. I find that if I then hang the piece up somewhere dry, out of direct sunlight for a couple of weeks, the curing process helps to extend the life of the colours. You may find that some colours are fugitive and change over time, while others are more reliable and last for years in the same state. In any case, the longer you leave the cloth to cure before washing it, the longer the colours will last.

5. After curing, the fabric can be handwashed with some cool or lukewarm water and a gentle pH-neutral soap.

ice flower dyeing

Extracting colour from flowers can be difficult. You may find that applying heat to delicate petals disrupts their bright hues and causes a loss of colour. Using a cold extraction technique can be more successful, especially if you start by freezing the flowers – the drop in temperature causes the plant cells to naturally decompose, making it easier for the colour to pass through into the dye bath.

This is not a very colourfast way to dye fabrics, but it's a fun and easy method to overdye fabric in order to create layers of colours. When the colour of a dyed fabric fades, you can overdye using this technique to give it a fresh burst of vibrancy.

It's also a good way to get a second life out of used flowers from your home or garden, or waste flowers from the local florist. If they are wilting or slightly past their best, they are still fine to use for colour.

you will need
Plant material (fresh flowers and petals)
Netting bag or old tights (optional)
String
Freezer bag or airtight container
Pot or bowl
Fabric (washed, scoured, mordanted and pre-wetted)
Strainer
Press cloth
Steam iron
pH-neutral soap

plant material
Try deep-coloured flowers such as petunia and delphinium, or red rose and hollyhock.

fabric
This technique works best on silk (animal fibre) as it absorbs colours easily and holds onto them well.

mordant
For silk, use a mineral-based alum and cream of tartar mordant (see p31) to brighten the colours.

process
1. Put the fresh flowers and petals inside a netting bag, or pair of old tights tied with string – this is optional, but it helps you remove them from the container more easily. Next, place the flowers in a freezer bag or airtight container and freeze for at least 24 hours.

2. Fill a non-reactive pot or bowl with warm water. Take the frozen flowers out of the freezer and immediately submerge them in the warm water, before they have a chance to start defrosting.

3. Squeeze the flowers to encourage the colour to come out. You can do this for a few minutes until the water is full of colour.

4. Leave the flowers to sit in the water for a day or more to let the cold extraction continue. Alternatively, apply gentle heat to the dye bath for around 30 minutes, or until the water reaches a deep enough shade.

5. When you have a sufficient amount of colour, strain the plant material out. To check the colour is deep enough, dip a spoon into the bowl – if it disappears, you have lots of colour.

6. Add the fabric to the dye bath and use either a cold dye method or a hot dye method (see pp52–53 and follow the guidelines below).

7. For a cold dye method leave the fabric in the bowl until the desired colour is achieved. For a hot dye method, apply gentle heat for around 30 minutes, or until the fabric reaches a deep enough shade.

8. After dyeing, remove the fabric and hang it out to air dry somewhere warm and dry and out of direct sunlight for several days or weeks – the longer you leave it, the better.

9. Once cured, iron the fabric with a press cloth. Then wash it with pH–neutral soap, rinse it with cool/lukewarm water and hang it out to air dry.

Cornflower, pansy and Japanese maple on silk

hapazome

Hapazome is a printing technique that allows you to create unusual patterns and colour quickly, using nothing but a mallet. Since it often employs fugitive plant colours, it's good to use it for craft projects that are less concerned with colourfastness and work well as temporary items – such as a beautiful gift card or biodegradable wrapping paper made from unbleached recycled paper and local botanical colours.

I recommend trying this technique out on some scraps of cloth or paper similar to the one you will use for your final piece to get an idea of the best pressure and amount of hammering to use. With practice, you will learn how much is enough. You don't want to hammer it so much that the plant material becomes pulp and sticks to the fabric or paper. On the other hand, you need to do it hard enough to get a good impression.

you will need
Plant materials (fresh petals and leaves)
Card or paper, to protect the printing material
Fabric (washed, scoured and mordanted) or recycled paper to print on
Rubber mallet
Steam iron
Press cloth

plant material
My favourites to use are elegantly shaped Japanese maple and herb robert leaves, tiny violas and cute clovers – but I go for whatever I find around me at the time. Many flowers provide exciting bright colours, such as magenta and violet, but these change and soften over time – tree mallow flowers, for example, give a gentle purple pink that fades away within just a few weeks. Some common and wild flower petals and seed buds are known for reliable colour, including roses, cornflowers, buddleia, marigolds, chamomile, daisies, heather, petunias and geraniums. Experiment with other plant materials, such as berries, roots, leaves – and even food waste, such as onion skins, carrot tops, purple cabbage ends and kale or chard leaves.

fabric
I've used a soft woven satin silk (animal fibre) for this project as it takes up colours readily. For a similar result, try a silk such as habotai or crêpe de chine. You can also try plant fibres such as finely woven linen or calico.

mordant
If you're using silk, mordant with mineral-based alum and cream of tartar, see p31. For linen or calico, use the two-step mineral-based oak gall with alum and soda ash, see p34. Though the latter won't yield such bright results.

process
1. To prepare the flowers and leaves, snip the stem away from the base so you have relatively flat plant material. You can also press them in a flower press or between two heavy books.

2. Find a strong surface to work on, such as a stone floor. Lay some card or paper down as protection.

3. Put the fabric or paper down on the surface, and place the plant materials on top. I've created a mirror image for this project – to do this, fold the cloth or paper over the top of the plant material, so you get two prints from the same items. If you don't want a mirror image, place some scrap fabric or paper over the plant materials.

4. Using the rubber mallet, gently bash the surface until the colour comes through, and you have sufficiently pressed all the botanicals. Once you're happy, gently shake or peel off the plant material.

5. Hang the fabric out to air dry for a few days, away from direct sunlight. Usually, the longer you leave it, the more substantive the colours will be.

6. As this is not the most permanent printing technique, it's a good idea to treat your prints gently. Prolong their life by steam pressing the fabric with an iron and press cloth before delicately handwashing with cool water and pH-neutral soap and air drying.

indigo vat dyeing

Indigo is a vat dye and unlike other natural dyes, it is not soluble in water. Instead it is soluble in an alkaline environment from which the oxygen has been removed.

Extracting indigo from its plant origin requires a complex fermentation process, which is labour and time intensive.

It has to be extracted in water in its colourless 'indican' state, fermented, and finally mixed with lime and pressed into cakes.

For centuries, indigenous cultures have dyed with indigo using a fermentation vat technique that is a skilled art. It takes at least ten days to prepare the vat before you can use it, and once ready it takes an experienced dyer to keep it balanced and in a dyeable state. Any irregularities can imbalance the vat and set the process back several days before it can proceed again.

Thankfully a simplified method was developed by French chemist and natural dyer Michel Garcia that uses just three natural ingredients: slaked lime, fructose sugar and indigo. This technique has been adopted by dyers around the world and is the basis of the instructions here.

Indigo has a wonderful history. Its name may derive from one of the oldest civilisations in the world, that of the Indus Valley in India. The Greek word *indikon* literally translates as 'Indian dye' or 'Indian', which later became 'indigo' in English. Indigo is one of the most ancient and rarest of natural dye colours – a cuneiform tablet from Mesopotamia dating back to 600 BC features a recipe for a layered blue dye. Indigo was used as a pigment for making paints, medicines and cosmetics by the ancient Egyptians and Romans, for medieval manuscript illuminations, and in masterpieces by artists such as Rubens during the late 16th to early 17th centuries.

Around 50 of the 200 or so indigo-bearing plants grow in India, the earliest major centre of natural indigo production. From there it was exported in the form of small cakes, which in 300–400 AD the Greeks and Romans believed were composed of precious minerals. It was not until the 13th century that Marco Polo returned from his journey to Asia to enlighten Europeans that indigo was a plant-based product. In the 19th century, indigo was known as 'blue gold' and was the ideal trading commodity: it travelled well and had a long life span, and it was compact, highly valued and rare.

Indigo refers to the dye compound contained within indigo-bearing plants. One of the most commonly used commercially for obtaining indigo dye is *Indigofera tinctoria*. Japanese indigo (*Persicaria tinctorium*) is another popular variety. In South and Central America you will find anil (*Indigofera suffruticosa*) and in Europe, our native species, although somewhat paler in colour, is woad.

Woad has a lower concentration of indigo, so local woad industries were threatened when imported indigo began to arrive from India in huge quantities. In response some governments laid down harsh rules from the 16th to early 17th century to outlaw the use of Asian indigo, naming it 'the devil's dye', and the 'false and pernicious Indian drug'. Indigo does have something of a dark history: the East India Company manipulated Indian farmers into switching from growing food crops, which communities relied on, to growing valuable indigo crops for export. But the farmers only received a tiny 2.5% of the market value of the indigo and quickly went into debt. This led to a huge 'indigo revolt' in 1859, in which many peasants were slaughtered.

The burgeoning fashion industry of the 19th century and the Industrial Revolution, along with the popularity of Levi's jeans, demanded vast quantities of blue-dyed cloth. This spurred the development of a synthetic replacement for indigo by German chemist Adolf von Baeyer during the 1880s. Following this, both the natural indigo and woad industries collapsed. Today, only some small-scale natural indigo farming exists, for artisan natural dyers.

you will need
Rubber gloves, face mask and goggles
Indigo
Slaked lime (calcium hydroxide)
Fructose sugar
Scales or measuring spoons
Large bowl
Mug or old jar
Measuring cups
Heat source
Bain-marie-style bowl inside a pot
Thermometer
Long-handled spoon
Dye vat (pot)
pH-neutral soap

indigo
Remember that powdered indigo is a precious dye material, extremely valuable and rare – so be careful to avoid wasting any pigment during the dyeing process. You can buy indigo online – look for organically grown and processed varieties. It comes as a deep blue powder and is expensive. As a rough guide, you'll need 25g (⅞oz) of indigo powder, 50g (1¾oz) of slaked lime and 75g (2⅝oz) of fructose to dye around 500g (18oz) of washed, scoured and dry fabric a medium to deep blue colour.

slaked lime and fructose
I use slaked lime (calcium hydroxide) to create the alkaline solution. Slaked lime is made when lime or quicklime (calcium oxide) is mixed, or 'slaked', with water. It has many names, including hydrated lime, caustic lime, builders' lime, slack lime or pickling lime. You can get it from builders' merchants or some DIY shops.

The slaked lime has to be reduced, using fructose (a sugar) to remove excess oxygen from the solution. You can buy fructose (which comes as crystals) in whole food shops or some supermarkets.

fabric
I've used a 100% organic and natural cotton (plant fibre) for this project. You can use any light or medium weight plant fibre.

mordant
Indigo doesn't require a mordant, which saves time, energy and water in comparison to most other types of dyeing.

safety
Slaked lime (calcium hydroxide) is a strong alkaline, and prolonged exposure may cause severe skin irritation, chemical burns, blindness and lung damage. It's extremely important to observe proper safety measures when preparing and using the vat. Avoid prolonged contact with skin, prevent splashes from getting in your eyes and do not swallow any dye materials. Protect your hands with thick waterproof gloves and cover your eyes with protective goggles.

Be careful to avoid inhaling dust particles when handling powders. Wear a dust mask, and work in a well-ventilated area. Store all ingredients in clearly labelled containers, out of reach of children and pets.

If disposing of spent solutions, do so responsibly, by diluting with plenty of water and pouring onto waste land (after asking the landowner) or flushing into the sewage system.

preparing the vat

1. Measure out the required amount of indigo powder using the measuring spoons or scales in a ratio of 1 part indigo, to 2 parts slaked lime (calcium hydroxide) and 3 parts fructose. As an example, to dye 500g (18oz) of fabric a medium to deep blue you'll need 25g (⅞oz) of indigo, 50g (1¾oz) of slaked lime and 75g (2⅝oz) of fructose.

2. For your vat, use a large steel mixing bowl, or other non-reactive container. Mix a tiny amount of warm water with the indigo powder – just enough to make a paste.

3. Using a mug or old jar, stir in 1 to 2 cups of warm water (around 43–50°C or 109–122°F) and blend to a smooth consistency. Add the fructose bit by bit, stirring it in until it has dissolved.

4. Start to slowly add the slaked lime – a bit at a time, not all at once – stirring well and smoothing out any clumps with each addition. Note that adding the slaked lime can create heat and it has a tendency to lump together, creating more heat, so it's best to work out any clumps quickly. Adding slaked lime may also cause bubbling and overflowing, so add it gradually and with great care.

5. Once you have a smooth consistency and all the lumps have been worked out, add enough warm water to fill the vat to about 5cm (2in) below the top rim. Stir around carefully in a clockwise motion, allowing the mixture to swirl into a circular vortex and the bubbles to collect in the centre. This collection of bubbles is called the 'indigo flower'.

6. Leave the dye to settle. Once settled the indigo flower should appear blue, with no white flecks. Let it sit for 30 minutes to 1 hour. During this time, the liquid will start reducing: the sugar is causing a chemical reaction that causes the oxygen to leave the solution.

7. After this time, take a clean stainless steel spoon and dip below the surface of the liquid to check its colour. It should no longer appear dark blue or greeny-blue – instead, it should be a clear liquid with an amber, yellow, greeny-yellow, yellow-brown or yellow-red colour (depending on the type of indigo used). If you are using a transparent glass vat, you will see a layer of sediment on the bottom. If the liquid does not appear to be changing colour yet, but the edges of the surface appear to be a clear yellow, this is an indication that the process is happening and it just needs a little more time.

8. If it remains a thick blue colour, carefully stir again in a clockwise circular motion as before, making sure you are mixing the bottom layer of sediment with the top layer. Then stand the vat in a bain-marie or similar, and heat it up to 50–60°C (122–140°F) for 30 minutes to help the process along. Always use a bain-marie as the indigo shouldn't be heated over a direct heat at this stage.

9. The dye is ready for use when the liquid has changed colour as described in step 7, has a dark blue indigo flower (the collection of bubbles on the top) and an iridescent coppery scum on the surface (a bit like a petrol spill).

10. When you feel you have the desired result, give the mixture a careful stir and top with more hot water (50–60°C or 122–140°F), filling the vat, but leaving a few centimetres/inches at the top to allow you to submerge the fabric without the indigo spilling out. You should see it start to take on a murky yellow-green hue and within about 30 minutes it should have reduced again.

11. After this time, check to see if you have the same signals again: the blue indigo flower, the coppery scum, and a transparent yellowish liquid below the surface. Once this stage is complete, you can start the dyeing.

From top left: adding fructose; stirring out the lumps;
indigo 'flower'; yellowish liquid

Bain-marie on a hot plate

dyeing

1. The vat has two layers. The upper layer is the transparent yellowish solution – this is the dye solution and where the fabric should stay when dyeing. The bottom area is the sediment, which you need to keep separate from the dye solution. Be careful not to let the cloth go too far down into the vat, where it may touch the bottom layer of sediment. This can lead to uneven colouring, and encourages the sediment to mix into the upper layer, which could cause the vat to unbalance – in which case you will have to go back and balance it again. If your vat is large enough, try placing a plastic laundry basket above the sediment and fastened to the top of the vat to act as a protective barrier. This will allow your hands to move more freely without worrying about how deep the fabric has gone.

2. When you're ready to dye, remove the indigo flower from the surface of the vat using a spoon or sieve.

3. Keep an eye on the temperature of the vat – you want it to stay between 30 and 60°C (86 and 140°F) while dyeing. If it starts to get too hot, turn off the heat. It won't necessarily damage the indigo if it overheats (though it might get too much for gloved hands), but if it's too cold, you will not be able to dye.

4. Wearing protective gloves, put the pre-wetted fabric slowly into the vat, submerging it completely in one motion. It's important that it doesn't get dipped, come up, and then go back under again, because this will introduce extra oxygen into the vat.

5. Keep the fabric submerged for about 30 seconds, massaging it to encourage the dye to enter the fibres evenly. Don't keep the fabric submerged for long periods as this may stop the dye from attaching to it properly, impacting colourfastness.

6. Bring the fabric out of the vat, again all in one motion, but only so it hovers slightly above the surface of the liquid. This is so that any drips do not have to travel too far before hitting the liquid, which again limits the amount of oxygen entering the vat.

7. Indigo dye is expensive, so it's important to reduce the amount of waste. With the piece of cloth still hanging in one hand just above the liquid, slowly squeeze it from top to bottom so any excess dye liquid goes back into the vat. This also makes it easier for the indigo dye in the cloth to oxidise, as the oxygen can get to the fibre more easily.

8. Open up the cloth and watch as it turns from green to blue in front of your eyes. This is the oxidising process and the final element of the dye chemistry. Be aware of any areas that need to be opened up more fully to expose the dye to oxygen. Wait until the cloth is entirely blue and no greeny areas remain before continuing.

further dyeing

1. After the first dip, rinse the cloth in a bowl of clean water (reserving this for later rinses). If you are doing multiple dips, you'll need to rinse in this bowl after every third dip. Wring out any excess water before reintroducing the cloth to the vat.

2. Indigo is a layered dye and it will take several dips to achieve a medium to dark colour. Experiment with samples of cloth to find out how many dips, and how long the dip times need to be, to achieve the shade you want. Some dark blues will require 15–20 dips.

3. Keep following the dyeing steps until you reach the shade you want. Remember the item will look darker when wet: once it's washed and dried, it will be much lighter – you will get a knack for this with experience.

post-dyeing

1. Rinse the fabric with lukewarm water, wash with pH-neutral soap, then rinse again. Do this three times, or until the rinse water runs clean.

2. Hang the fabric to air dry, out of direct sunlight.

balancing the vat / troubleshooting

Since indigo is not soluble in water, the amount of water used in the process is minimal. And once in the vat, it stays there – it doesn't need to be removed as the vat can be balanced by adding more dye ingredients to allow for more dyeing. In fact, the vat lasts forever – you simply keep balancing it by topping it up with more indigo, slaked lime or fructose – or all three if need be.

If you have followed the steps correctly, and have both an indigo flower and a coppery scum but the liquid is still dark blue, try stirring in 1 tbsp of fructose to encourage the reduction to occur and the colour to change.

If you've tried the previous suggestion and it hasn't changed colour after 30 minutes, and you still have the indigo flower and copper scum, you may need to wait longer or add more fructose. Try giving it another stir and waiting 15 minutes. If this still does nothing, stir in another teaspoon of fructose.

If you have no indigo flower or coppery scum, stir in 1 tbsp of slaked lime.

If you have no indigo flower, but you do have blue bubbles and a coppery scum, this is still okay – the bubbles may just have dispersed.

If the dye liquid turns blue, it needs to be rebalanced by stirring in 1 tbsp of slaked lime and 2 tbsp of fructose and waiting 30 minutes. It should then turn a transparent yellowish colour again. If not, try applying some heat or follow the troubleshooting tips above.

If you keep dipping and see no deepening of the colour, you may have used up the indigo, so you will need to add more. Follow the ratio in step 1 to measure out the right quantity for the amount of cloth you have. Add the extra indigo to the vat by first mixing it with water to make a paste, then a liquid, and then carefully adding that to the vat. Stir the whole vat with a long-handled spoon and wait for it to settle, before following the dyeing steps again.

indigo chart

The photograph on the right shows the number of dips needed to achieve various shades of blue. The fabric is organic cotton (plant fibre). From the top:

0	dips
1	dips
3	dips
6	dips
12	dips
18	dips
24	dips

shibori

Shibori is an ancient Japanese dyeing technique, used to create repeat patterns by compressing areas of fabric using wooden blocks, string, clamps or a range of found objects, which then prevent the dye from penetrating and therefore stop – or resist – that area of fabric from being dyed.

The name comes from the Japanese 'shiboru', which refers to a method of wringing or squeezing laundry. The earliest known example of the technique dates back to the 8th century, when the main fabrics available were only cotton, hemp and silk. Indigo was the dye of choice, although some dyers also used madder and beetroot.

There are many different shibori techniques and types of equipment, making a diverse range of designs. With *arashi shibori*, cloth is wrapped around a long pole and string is wound over it to create small creases, then the fabric is pushed down the pole to squash it together at one end. This gives wonderful wavy water-like impressions. *Itajimi shibori* requires a pair of shaped objects, traditionally made from wood, which are placed on either side of a concertina-folded cloth and compressed with string to resist the dye. *Kanoko shibori* is what we commonly refer to as 'tie-dye' in the West – it involves binding areas with thread to create circle shapes in the cloth.

There is a correct way to use shibori techniques and precision is typically part of its tradition. However, there are a thousand ways that you can adapt the forms and materials, and much beauty is to be found in the inconsistencies and mistakes! There are an infinite number of ways you can bind, fold and stitch cloth to achieve different patterns. You may find some techniques suit certain kinds of fabric better than others, and you can also use more than one style together, to create even more intricate designs. And you can experiment with using any kind of natural dye colour. These pages demonstrate a couple of simple and elegant shibori techniques for you to try.

you will need
Fabric (washed, scoured and mordanted)
Steam iron
Press cloth
2 square wooden blocks
C-clamps/market clips
String
Tongs
Indigo vat or dye bath
pH-neutral soap

fabric
I've used a 100% organic and natural cotton (plant fibre) for this project. You can use any light- or medium-weight plant fibre to achieve a similar look. But you can experiment with any tightly woven animal or plant fibre.

mordant
I've used indigo vat dyeing for this project, so no mordant was necessary. If you're using a different dye bath, use the correct mordant for your fibre – see pp28–34.

dye

If you're making a dye bath (rather than using indigo vat dyeing), opt for a good rich colour such as madder, cochineal, logwood or sappanwood.

itajimi shibori – square concertina

1. With this technique you fold the fabric concertina-style into a square, which yields a design with a grid of squares. Make sure you have followed the appropriate scouring and mordanting instructions for the fabric you are working with.

2. Lay the piece of cloth out on the work surface and iron out any creases. You will be folding the fabric like an accordion or concertina and clamping the block around it to leave a small margin/border around the edge – it is this area that will be dyed. So start by placing one of the wooden blocks on one corner to gauge/measure how many folds you can make in the cloth, while still leaving a small margin around the block. If you want a really neat finish and a complete grid print (no half grids), then trim the fabric to size.

3. Concertina-fold the cloth from one end to the other, making equal-sized folds so you end up with a narrow length of folded fabric. You can give the folds a press with a steam iron for a more immaculate finish, or leave unpressed for a more rustic look.

4. Take the long length of folded cloth and fold it in half from one end to the other.

5. Then concertina-fold it (or fold it back on itself) until you are left with a square shape. Press these folds too if you wish.

6. Place the folded square between the two wooden blocks so there is an equal margin of fabric left exposed the whole way around the blocks.

7. Position the clamp in the middle of the blocks, so that they are tightly compressing the folds.

8. Now submerge the whole thing in water and leave it to soak overnight, or for at least an hour, to pre-wet it before dyeing.

9. This project was done with indigo vat dyeing, and was dipped about 20 times. You can use any preferred dye bath. Leave the folded piece to dye in the bath using the hot or cold method that's appropriate to the fabric and dye. You may need to weigh the piece down with something heavy to stop it from floating to the top. Gently move it around every now and then to make sure it is not touching any other surfaces, and is receiving the dye fully all over the exposed areas.

post-dyeing

1. When you have finished dyeing, remove the fabric from the indigo vat and allow to cool. Carefully unfold the fabric and hang it out to air dry.

2. If you have used another dye bath, remove the fabric from the dye bath and allow it to air dry out of direct sunlight. Leave to cure for a few days or weeks – the longer the better. After it's cured, wash the fabric with pH-neutral soap. Finish setting the dye by giving the fabric a final steam with a steam iron and a press cloth.

printing inks
for woodblock printing

you will need
Plant-based binder powder – I've used gum tragacanth
Measuring cup
Bowls
Spoon
Electric blender (optional)
Extract powder – I've used logwood

extract powder
Be aware that gum tragacanth (plant-based binder powder) has an acidic pH, which will affect the colour outcomes of your printing inks. In this case, I've used logwood (traditionally purple/blue), but after adding gum tragacanth, the ink becomes orange.

plant-based binder powder
You can transform natural dyes into inks suitable for woodblock printing by using a plant-based binder, such as gum tragacanth, gum arabic or any other plant starch – including cornflour (cornstarch), potato starch, wheat starch and so on. Consider which crops grow locally that you can extract starch from, or buy it online as a powder.

mordant
If you are printing onto paper, you are unlikely to need a mordant to fix the dye colours, as colourfastness in the wash won't be an issue. Simply choose a dye that has good lightfastness and so does not fade over time. If you are printing onto fabric, you may wish to use a mordant to fix the colours well. You can pre-mordant the fabric as usual, or you can add the mordant (in this case alum powder) to the printing ink before using it. If you choose this option, you need to work quickly and add the mordant at the last minute, as the mordant is at risk of bonding with the pigment rather than the fibre. Also, a mordanted ink can only be stored for one day.

process
Use ½ tsp of plant-based binder powder to 240ml (8½ fl oz) boiling water. This is sufficient for several prints. Scale these quantities up to suit larger projects.

1. Measure the required amount of plant-based binder powder and boiling water into a bowl. Mix well with a spoon or in an electric blender (that's reserved for dyeing) until all the lumps have disappeared.

2. Leave the mixture to thicken overnight in the fridge.

3. The next day, mix 1 tsp of extract powder with a few drops of hot water to make a paste, and then a few more to create a liquid consistency – use the least amount of water possible, so as not to dilute the colour too much.

4. Mix the liquid colour with 120ml (4¼ fl oz) of the binder mixture from the fridge – again you can mix by hand or use a blender.

5. Bear in mind that colours will appear much lighter once dry and washed. For darker colours, use a higher ratio of extract powder to binder.

adding a mordant to ink
First follow steps 1–5, but using different quantities. Use 1 tsp binder to 240ml (8½ fl oz) boiling water.

Next, make a small quantity of mordant solution using 1 tsp alum powder with the smallest amount of boiling water possible to dilute completely. Ideally only 1–2 tsp of water.

Once dissolved, add the mordant solution to the ink and blend well by hand or with an electric blender.

Use this mordanted ink quickly for your printing. It's best not to store it for longer than a day.

woodblock printing

Woodblock printing is a traditional relief technique. It uses a wooden block with an image carved into it to apply motifs and patterns to textile and paper surfaces. Tools are used to carve an image into the block's surface of the block, removing areas that will not be printed. The technique described in these pages uses a water-based printing ink, with a plant starch mixed into it. This is inspired by traditional Japanese and Chinese woodblock printing, which uses rice starch as a binder. The similar practice of Western woodcut often uses oil-based inks.

Traditional Japanese woodblock printing uses thin Japanese plywood, but any local, sustainably grown softwood can be used. Pine, cedar and cypress are a bit too soft, and can compress while printing and therefore don't transfer images so well. Harder woods can be used, but they are more difficult to carve and require sharper cutting tools and consistent tool sharpening. I tend to use a cherry plywood, which has a thin layer of cherry wood on a plywood stack of birch wood, which is great for holding finely detailed designs. You can also try mahogany, poplar, ash, birch, apple or wood from any other fruit tree.

you will need
Pencil and paper/tracing paper for drawing design (optional)
Woodblocks (one for each colour)
Non-slip mat or wooden bench hook
Woodblock carving tools
Water mister
Inks (see recipes on p121)
Paint brush
Sponge
Paper or fabric (washed, scoured and mordanted)
Baren (for pressing with, optional)
Steaming equipment
pH-neutral soap

ink
The printing ink recipe is on p121. Here I've used logwood extract powder with gum tragacanth binder.

wood
The wood should be clean, well seasoned or kiln dried, and perfectly flat.

A thickness of 0.6cm (¼ in) to 7.5cm (3 in) works well. The thicker the wood, the less it will bend.

I would avoid using MDF (medium density fibreboard) as it contains toxic glues, with formaldehyde and other harmful chemicals, which are damaging to health when handled or inhaled while carving. They can also dull the colour of inks.

My print design has only one colour, so I only need one block. If you wish to use more colours, you will need an additional block for each colour. You can use double-sided woodblocks and have an image on each side, to minimise the amount you buy or waste.

carving
Work on a non-slip surface or wooden bench hook that fits against the side of the work surface, to keep the block steady while you carve. Always carve away from your body. Hold the gouging tools like a pencil, and the knife tool with your four fingers wrapped around, and thumb on top of the upright end.

I have used Japanese wood-carving tools. It's important to invest in good-quality, sharp and comfortable-to-grip tools, and I find these wood-handled tools are best. The difference between using them and cheap plastic options is huge. You can buy them online, and they do last if you look after them. Sharpen them often, ideally after every use.

fabric or paper
I've used habotai silk (animal fibre) for this project. You can use any tightly woven animal or plant fibre.

mordant
If you are using silk, mordant it using mineral-based alum and cream of tartar mordant, see p31. Or use the correct mordant for your fabric – see pp28–34.

If you're using paper, prepare it before printing by spraying each sheet lightly using a water mister. Stack the sheets on top of each other, with a piece of dry paper above and below the stack, then wrap in a plastic bag and leave overnight. This allows the ink to be absorbed into the paper when printing.

process

1. Draw your design directly onto the wooden block if you feel confident. If not, sketch it on some paper first, then transfer it using tracing or carbon paper.

2. Begin to cut into the block, using the knife tool first to trace the outline of the motif. The line should remain visible as you are cutting along the side of it.

3. When you have finished cutting around the line, take the smallest gouging tool in your kit and, working close to the line, start to carve away from the knife cut. Use a shallow stroke to begin clearing the wood around the line drawing and work for a couple of strokes outwards from the line.

4. Now switch to a medium gouging tool to carve a bit further out from the line. Finally, use the largest gouging tool to carve the rest (or most) of the surface off the block, so that only the line drawing design is in relief on the board.

5. When the block is ready to use, it's good to practise your printing technique a few times on some scrap paper or cloth, to experiment with how you apply pressure, the amount of ink you use and how you load it onto the block. This may differ with each kind of surface you print onto.

6. Lightly mist the block with water to allow it to hold the ink. Then use a brush to load a layer of ink onto it. Make sure the ink is spread evenly by using a forward and backward motion, so no brush marks are visible. Wipe any excess ink off the sides of the print area with a sponge to give a crisp line.

7. Take a piece of dampened paper or fabric, and lay it flat on the work surface. Place the inked-up block onto the print surface, applying light pressure and using a circular motion to rub the back of the block, but being careful not to move it around. A few strong taps with the fleshy side of your hand may also give a good effect. If you have a baren, you can use this instead, applying light pressure in circular motions.

8. Lift the block up off the surface evenly with one hand, using the other hand to hold the cloth or paper down so all areas of the block come off at the same time.

9. You can keep on printing as many times as you like by repeating the same process. When you reload the block with ink using the brush, be careful to wipe down the sides so there are no unwanted splodges or marks.

post-printing

1. Wash your tools with water and some pH-neutral soap and let them air dry.

2. Hang the paper or fabric to air dry on a rack, out of direct sunlight, and leave to cure for a few days, or for a couple of weeks if possible. The longer you can let the ink set in and cure, the longer the dye will last.

3. If you are printing onto fabric, you will need to steam the print to set the colour once it's dry. I use a bullet steamer to do this for 1 hour. If you don't have access to a bullet steamer, you can fashion a makeshift steamer out of a stainless steel pot, with a strainer inside and a lid. Or you can use a regular steam iron for 20 minutes at a time, until you've been steam ironing for 1 hour in total.

4. For all steaming, place the dry print onto a layer of calico and place another layer of calico fabric on top. Roll up into a sausage shape and carefully place inside the steamer. The calico protects the ink from smudging and leaching onto other areas of the fabric. Calico is breathable, so allows the steam to pass through. It's also cheaper than other fabrics.

5. Hang to air dry out of direct sunlight and allow to cure for a day or so. Then press with an iron and press cloth.

6. Wash the fabric with warm water and pH-neutral soap, then air dry and press it with an iron. Any further washing should also be done in this way, to preserve the integrity of the natural dyes.

drawing ink

When I think of natural drawing ink, my mind wanders to medieval Britain, to old parchment paper and wax sealed scrolls, to secret messages, Robin Hood and letters between Shakespearean star-crossed lovers. It's easy to make and could bring a touch of romance to your drawing and letter writing.

The word ink is derived from the Latin *encaustus*, which literally means 'burned in'. The tannic acid used in traditional ink recipes burns the top layer of the paper or parchment when it is applied, while the pigment sits on top of the surface layer, much like a paint. There are countless recipes for making ink, which can be adapted and added to as you go, allowing you to adjust to differences in surface qualities and textures.

I've given two recipes for you to try. One is a simple ink recipe that you can make with many substantive dye plant materials to create a range of colours. The other is a traditional indelible ink recipe, which contains iron to deepen the colours to give black hues and leave a permanent mark. It's an oak gall ink, which would once have been used with a quill or, later, a dipping pen. You can see it on historical manuscripts, though some have suffered damage as a result of the acidity of the tannic acid in the oak galls, which eats away at natural fibres such as paper or parchment over time.

You can use these inks for drawing with a quill, dipping pen, or any other kind of writing tool, such as a stick or brush.

binders and inks

Both inks use a binder to thicken the ink and make it suitable for writing or drawing. In these recipes, I use gum arabic (see below), which is a natural resin extracted from the acacia tree that is solid and translucent orange in colour. It aids the consistency of the ink, acting as a binder and creating an even dispersion of pigment.

You may wish to adapt the ink and vary the type and quantity of binder to suit your needs. The paper you write on, the work surface you rest on, and the tool you use to draw with can all alter the way the ink flows from pen to paper.

You can experiment with different binder pastes to see which works best with your choice of plant colour. Egg white, oils, potato, wheat, cornflour (cornstarch) and even honey are good options.

gum arabic solution

This is a binder used in making some paints. You can buy gum arabic powder online or from art shops – it can come in rock form and needs to be ground into a powder before use.

To make a gum arabic solution, mix 3 parts of boiling water to 1 part of gum arabic powder. Mix this by hand, continually stirring for 10–15 minutes. Don't do this in a blender, as it tends to whip up and cause bubbles. The solution should be quite thick. To finish, weigh the solution, and add 25% of its weight in runny honey – acacia honey is ideal, as it comes from the same acacia tree as gum arabic.

simple drawing ink

you will need
Dye powder or plant material
Measuring cup or spoons
Gum arabic solution (see p126)
Salt
Vinegar

Additional items for plant material process:
Scales
Heat source (optional)
Pot
Sieve

dye powder or plant material

This process begins with extracting colour from local, seasonal plants and waste foods to create a dye bath with the smallest amount of water possible, and then reducing this down to a concentrate. Mix in a binder and a preservative to make an ink.

I've used cochineal dye powder, but you can use any fresh, dry or frozen plant material, or other dye powder. Chopped beetroot, avocado rinds, coffee grounds, tea leaves, berries, eucalyptus, nettle leaves, dock and dandelion root or any other dye plant are all interesting options.

process: powder

1. Mix 1 tsp dye powder with about 2 tsp water – you want to make a paste with the smallest amount of water possible.

2. Add 1 tsp of the gum arabic solution to the paste.

3. To preserve the ink, add 1 tsp clear white vinegar and 1 tsp salt.

process: plant material

1. Place 500g (18oz) of plant material (such as nettle) in a pot and add 500ml (1 pint) of water, or enough just to cover the plant material. It's key to use the smallest amount of water possible.

2. To use a quick hot extraction technique, apply heat and bring to a gentle simmer. Simmer for 30 minutes to an hour.

3. To use a more environmentally friendly cold extraction technique, cover the pot with a lid and leave for several weeks, or until the water has turned dark in colour.

4. For both options, once you have a good amount of colour in the water, strain the dye bath with a sieve to remove the plant material.

5. Place the pot over a low heat, and reduce the liquid until you have a thick, syrup-like consistency and the colour saturation you prefer.

6. Add 1 tsp of gum arabic solution to your dye mixture.

7. To preserve the ink, add 1 tsp clear white vinegar and 1 tsp salt.

indelible drawing ink

you will need

This recipe makes about 500ml (1 pint) of ink.

56g (2oz) whole oak galls, or oak gall powder
Pestle and mortar/hammer (optional)
Grinder (optional)
Scales
Rain water or distilled water
Cheesecloth
30g (1oz) ferrous sulphate powder
15g (½oz) gum arabic solution (see p126)
Ink well, for storage

oak gall

While oak gall was the ingredient of choice in old European inks, walnut was also used, so try it as an alternative in this recipe to create a brown/black ink. For more on oak galls, see p33.

ferrous sulphate

Also known as copperas or green vitriol, this is a synthesised metallic salt that you can obtain as blue-green crystals or as a white powder.

process

1. Crush the dried oak galls with a pestle and mortar – or with a hammer in a drying bag – until you have very small lumps. Then grind them to a powder using a grinder. If you've bought oak gall powder, skip straight to the next step.

2. Add 56g (2oz) of oak gall powder to 500ml (1 pint) water. Leave to soak for 24 hours.

3. Strain the oak gall liquid through the cheesecloth.

4. Mix the ferrous sulphate into the strained solution.

5. Finally, add the gum arabic solution and stir well.

6. Store in a glass ink well with a cork stopper – this not only makes it look good, but also keeps it fresh and safe. Storing it in the fridge makes it last even longer.

eco-printing with leaves

There are many ways to approach eco-printing with leaves. This partial process uses a selection of local windfall autumn leaves – oak, maple and eucalyptus – together with plant-fibre fabric – organic unbleached cotton – pre-mordanted with iron (ferrous sulphate solution). I dampen the leaves in water to soften them, before padding them dry and folding them into layers of the cloth that I then bind tightly around a wooden stick with string for steaming.

you will need
Fabric (washed, scoured and mordanted)
Leaves
String
Steaming equipment (for hot dyeing)
Tongs
Iron powder (ferrous sulphate) solution or homemade
iron water (see recipes on pp38–39)
Steam iron
Press cloth
pH-neutral soap

process
1. Soak the leaves in water to dampen and soften overnight. Pad dry with a tea towel or towel for crisp prints.

2. Take the pre-washed cotton fabric – a tight weave is best for a clear, crisp result – and pre-wet and pre-mordant by dipping it into an iron mordant solution (ferrous sulphate mixed with warm water). I add about a cupful to a small pot that I reserve solely for iron use. Always use gloves when handling iron and protect your eyes and airways with goggles and a mask. Iron taints dyes grey/black and can ruin results, so keep all iron equipment separate from other dye equipment and wash it separately.

3. Pad the fabric dry so it is damp rather than wet. Place the damp leaves in an arrangement to your liking on one half of the pre-mordanted fabric, and then fold the other half over the top of the leaves. This will create a mirror-image pattern – much like the butterfly prints you used to make at school.

4. Wrap the cloth tightly around a length of smooth round wood, such as a section of broom handle or a rolling pin. Fasten it tightly with a natural string or twine (see image).

5. Place inside your steamer – make sure the piece is the right size to fit inside the steaming vessel with the lid closed.

6. Steam for 1 hour, turning once to allow steam to penetrate over it all evenly.

7. Remove with tongs, being careful not to burn yourself on the steam or pot. Leave to cool before handling.

8. Undo the string and open the cloth. You should find some lovely leaf prints where the tannin in the leaves has reacted with the iron on your fibre to create colour-fast prints.

9. You can overlay your print with further prints to build up a collection of layers and ghostly silhouettes on your fabric. It can look very enchanting with more layers and depths of colour.

10. I suggest letting the pieces dry hanging up and then giving them a steam press with an iron and press cloth, before washing with gentle natural soap and warm water to rinse away the iron water.

I have used this technique to make some tea towels (see image).

6 projects

dip-dye gift tags

One of the simplest ways to add a touch of natural colour to presents is with pretty dip-dyed paper gift tags. You can make these any time you have a dye bath left over from another project. Also try experimenting with dyeing wrapping paper or greetings cards – add a woodblock print (see p122) or write your message in drawing inks (see pp126–129) for a completely natural-dyed gift wrap.

you will need
Dye material
Recycled paper tags
Small bowl
Water
Length of string
Pegs/hooks

dye material
Cochineal powder, see p63. About ¼ tsp of dye powder in a small bowl of water is enough for about 20 tags. Or use any dye bath solution left over from another project.

paper tags
Paper luggage labels or gift tags, ideally recycled. You can also try using recycled paper, such as Khadi paper from India, which is made from offcuts from the cotton textile industry – it has a brilliant texture.

dye method
Dye bath, cold dyeing method – see p52.

process
Dip each tag into the dye bath until you get the desired depth of colour – the ones shown here only took around 30 seconds. If you're using very robust tags, you can leave them in for as long as 12 hours if you want deeper shades.

Gently lift the dyed tags out of the dye bath and dip them briefly into a bath of clear water to rinse off any excess dye sitting on the surface. This ensures that only the true colour that has dyed the paper fibres is left behind.

Using pegs or hooks, attach the tags to a line of string to air dry. Be careful when handling them, as they are particularly fragile when wet, and the colours could smudge onto other surfaces.

Leave for 30 minutes, or until the tags are dry to the touch. For a deeper colour, repeat the process.

table linen

There's something special about using food waste to create beautiful, decorative table linen – and it makes a great conversation piece when you gather around the table with friends. Consider the range of colours you can create: rich bronze from onion skins, soft dusty pinks from avocado rinds and pits, purple from red cabbage ends, yellow from carrot tops, and an array of beige and greens from coffee grounds and various types of tea leaves.

Lengths of yellow onion-dyed linen, with soft edges, add a touch of romantic style. I love the rustic, crumpled look of freshly washed linen, but you can try any natural fabrics for making runners and napkins. You might also like to use larger swathes of fabric to make a full tablecloth or bed throw. Layer up different qualities of linen, from light, loose weave to thicker, heavier weights.

you will need
Tape measure
Dyed fabric
Fabric scissors
Iron and ironing board
Dressmaker's pins
Sewing machine
Sewing thread

dye material
Onion skins – see p71. You'll need 100% of the weight of the washed, scoured and dried fabric in skins – so for 500g (18oz) of fabric, you'll need 500g (18oz) of dry onion skins

fabric
Irish linen (plant fibre). You can also use organic cotton, which gives a similar rustic finish. Silk (animal fibre) is wonderful for a more romantic look.

mordant
For Irish linen, use two-step mineral oak gall, alum and soda ash mordant – see p34.

dye method
Dye bath, hot dyeing method – see p52. For a similar shade, leave the fabric in the dye bath on a simmer for 1 hour. Then take off the heat and leave in the dye bath overnight.

modifier
I haven't used a modifier in this project, but an acid such as lemon juice or light vinegar gives brighter hues.

process
Measure the table width or length, depending on where you want the runner to sit. A table runner looks good when it's about one third of the width of the table, and running down the middle lengthways. So if the table is 120cm (48in) wide, the runner should be 40cm (16in) wide. If you want to leave the runner in place for dinner parties, make sure there is enough space on each side of it for placemats without them overlapping the runner.

The length of the runner should overhang the ends of the table by about 15–25cm (6–10in) on each end. So, if the table is 175cm (70in) long, the table runner will be 190–200cm (75–80in) long.

Napkins are square, and can be any size from 40 x 40cm (16 x 16in) to 50 x 50cm (20 x 20in). Larger sizes tend to be for formal events, to be folded into shapes or around silverware.

When you've established what sizes you need, cut all the pieces from the fabric. I've left a rough, frayed hem as I like the rustic look. If you prefer a neater finish, allow 2cm (¾in) extra all round each piece for a hem.

Make a double hem by folding the edges of each piece under by 1cm (⅜in) to the wrong side and then fold under again by 1cm (⅜in). Press the folds with the iron and then pin into place, adding the pins at a right angle to the edge so that the needle can sew over them.

Using a sewing machine, sew the hem in place all round the edges, close to the first fold.

You could create a more elaborate design by using shibori dyeing techniques to add pattern to the cloth. For more on this, see pp117–118.

cushion cover

These scatter cushions are a great way to add natural colour to your home – their contrasting bright dye colours and sharp geometric shapes give them a contemporary feel.

you will need
Paper and pencil
30 x 30cm (12 x 12in) duck/goose feather or down cushion pad
Tape measure or ruler
Pieces of dyed fabric
Dressmaker's pins
Dressmaker's chalk
Fabric scissors
Sewing machine
Sewing threads in suitable colours
Iron and ironing board
2 pieces of 32 x 22cm (12½ x 8½in) plain cotton fabric

dye material
The pink is cochineal, see p63. The coral is madder, see pp64–65. The purple is logwood, see p82.

fabric
Organic cotton (plant fibre) – use a medium to heavyweight cotton with a tight weave. You could also use another plant fibre, such as linen. The project is ideal for using up scraps and offcuts.

mordant
For cotton, use two-step mineral oak gall, alum and soda ash mordant, see p34.

dye method
Dye bath, hot dyeing method. For cochineal, see p63. For madder, see pp64–65. For logwood, see p82.

process
Draw a 32 x 32cm (12½ x 12½in) square on the paper; this includes 1cm (⅜in) all round for the seam. Fill the square with a simple geometric design using squares and triangles.

Cut out the paper shapes and place them on the fabrics, pinning them down with some space between each one. Using dressmaker's chalk or a washable marker, mark a 1cm (⅜in) seam around each shape with a dotted line.

Cut the fabric shapes out along the dotted lines. Use the iron to steam press the seam to the reverse side all round each piece.

Arrange the fabric pieces into their correct positions, to see which ones need sewing together. Take two of the pieces and place them right sides together, with the edge to be sewn aligned. Use a sewing machine to sew a straight line along the pressed line. Press the seam open to reduce any bulkiness. Add the next pieces in the same way, until all the pieces are sewn together to create a full square.

Now make the envelope back for the cushion. On one long edge of each plain rectangular piece of fabric, fold under 3mm (⅛in), then fold under 7mm (¼in) to make a double hem. Use the sewing machine to sew each hem in place close to the first fold.

Now place one of the plain pieces flat, with the side that will be visible facing up and the hemmed edge on the right, then add the second piece on top, visible side facing up and hemmed edge on the left, so that the two hemmed edges overlap. Adjust the overlap to make the pieces into a 32 x 32cm (12½ x 12½in) square, then pin the two pieces securely together through the overlapping section.

Place the patchwork piece and the plain piece together, their visible sides both facing each other, with the edges aligned all round, and pin the layers together. Place the pins at a right angle to the edge so that the needle can sew over them.

Sew all round the edge with a sewing machine, taking a 1cm (⅜in) seam allowance all round. It's best to start in the middle of one side, sew to the corner, then pivot the piece on the needle so you can sew the next side – this gives a neat square corner. Repeat until you are back where you started, then backstitch for 2cm (¾in) to secure the end of the seam.

Remove the pins, turn the cushion cover right-side out and use something blunt to push out the corners into neat points. Press with the iron and insert the cushion pad to finish.

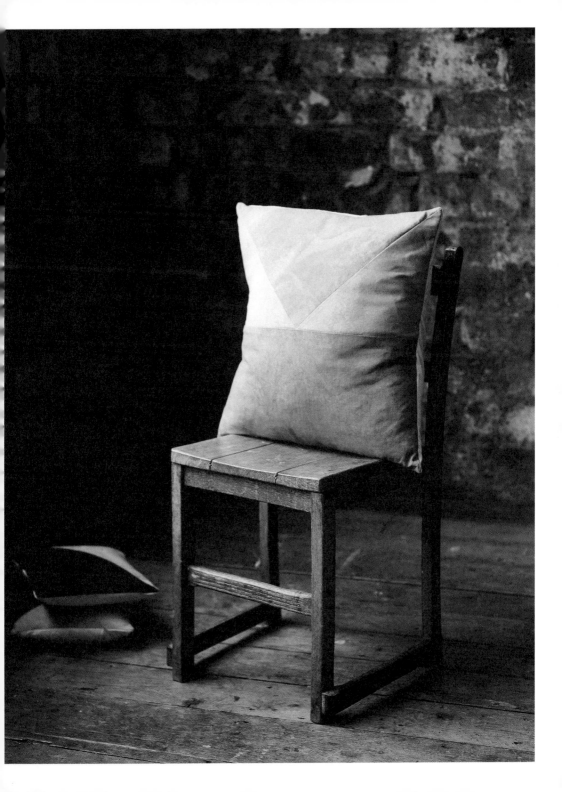

suppliers

natural dyes
UK
Botanical Inks – botanicalinks.com

USA
Botanical Colors – botanicalcolors.com
Aurora Silk – aurorasilk.com
Maiwa – maiwa.com/collections/natural-dyes

eco-cloth suppliers
UK
Botanical Inks – botanicalinks.com
Bristol Cloth – bristolcloth.co.uk
Bysshe – bysshe.com
Cloth House – clothhouse.com
Offset Warehouse – offsetwarehouse.com
Green Fibres – greenfibres.com
Organic Textile Co – organiccotton.biz/store

USA
Cloth Foundry – clothfoundry.com
Chico Flax – chicoflax.com
Huston Textile Company – hustontextile.com
Aurora Silk – aurorasilk.com
Vreseis (organic colour grown cotton) – vreseis.com

AUS
Beautiful Silks – beautifulsilks.com
Fibershed Directory – fibershed.org/producer-directory

eco-yarns
UK
Blacker Yarns – blackeryarns.co.uk
Tamarisk – tamariskfarm.co.uk
Cornish Organic Wool – cornishorganicwool.co.uk
Yarn Yarn – yarnyarn.co.uk

USA
The Woolery – woolery.com
Voices of Industry – voicesofindustry.com
Vreseis (organic colour grown cotton) – vreseis.com
Lani's Lana – lanislana.com
Fibershed Directory – fibershed.org/producer-directory

eco-paper suppliers
UK
Eco Craft (recycled) – eco-craft.co.uk
Shepherds (recycled and handmade) –
    store.bookbinding.co.uk
St Cuthberts Mill – stcuthbertsmill.com/st-cuthberts-
mill-paper/somerset-printmaking

USA
Eco Paper – ecopaper.com

traditional artist supplies
UK
L Cornelissen & Son – cornelissen.com

other useful and educational sites
Plants For A Future – pfaf.org
Fibershed – fibershed.com
Centre for Sustainable Fashion – sustainable-fashion.com
Cleaner Cotton – sustainablecotton.org
Textile Arts Center – textileartscenter.com
India Flint – indiaflint.com
Slow Fiber Studios – slowfiberstudios.com
Maiwa – maiwa.com/collections/natural-dyes
Botanical Colors – botanicalcolors.com

acknowledgements

I have so much gratitude for so many people who have been a part of my journey with natural dyes and this book.

Zena Alkayat, I am so grateful to you for providing me with the opportunity to write this book, and for bringing clarity to my words with your eloquence and clear vision. Your expertise in editing is so gracefully matched with your warmth and humour. Thank you for your commitment to this project and your faith in my work. And for bringing together the dream team for this co-creation.

Kim Lightbody, thank you for your beautiful photography, which has brought this book to life. Thank you Alexander Breeze for your sweet presence and charming style. Claire Rochford for shaping the visuals and flow so well. And to the whole editorial team at Quadrille who have poured over this text and polished the images to perfection.

I'm forever grateful to my family and friends who have nurtured and nourished me with love, care and guidance at every step.

Thank you Mum and Tonia for always being there and Dad for helping to make things happen! Mum – you were my original inspiration for living a sustainable life.

My dear Cassykins, for all of the years of friendship, and the hundreds of onion skins!

Emma Hague, your incredible work in sustainable textiles shines such hope and possibility on what we can do when we have a strong vision and work together to create it. You are a great connector of people, a visionary and a beautifully balanced force of intelligence and compassion. Working with you is such a blessing. Thank you for being an ongoing inspiration and ally.

Louise, you were the original illuminator of this path for me. I'm so grateful for this inspired and right-on introduction and for always showing up when I need you most.

Darling Petronella, thank you for being there and for such nurturing, inspirational, nourishing friendship, excellent ideas and general moving and shaking.

Ped, thank you for all your years of friendship and for always hosting me at the Palace!

Sophie HP, for all the gracious hosting throughout the months of crafting this book and for all of your support.

Sofia and Bridie, your gentle patience, support, spirit and sharing of space through this creative process have been so very appreciated.

Tom Beale, for all of the ways you have offered loving kindness and such generous support, I will always be grateful.

Tamara, for sharing your stories and your light.

For all of my teachers, mentors and colleagues who have shared so generously their wisdom, passion, insight and experience with me, in cultivating my understanding of natural materials.

Thank you to Rashid for guiding me into the ancient world of natural dyeing and printing, in what once was the Indus Valley. To Michael for sharing your home, purple potatoes and enchanting natural dyeing wisdom. David Cranswick for being such an inspiring and generous teacher. India Flint for being so true to your values. Cara Marie Piazza, for your fabulous witchcraft. Kathy Hattori, for your kind and generous support and just being such a beautiful soul. Jenny Dean, for lighting the way. Michel Garcia, for simplifying the organic indigo vat dyeing process and making it so accessible.

To my incredible community in Bristol, London and the wider field of sustainable textiles, design, craft, growing and farming. It's an honour and a delight to feel a sense of belonging among you all. And to be surrounded by such incredible visionaries, dreamers, innovators, doers and open-hearted folk.

Lizzie Harrison, for offering your wisdom and support. Dash + Miller, for your generous guidance and knowledge. Fernhill Farm, for being an inspiring wool partner. Old Market Manor, for providing the space for Botanical Inks to grow from. Charlotte and Ela, for your patience! Langfordians, thank you for so much ongoing support and providing space for making a mess. The Ethicurean, thank you for your kind support and encouragement. Mark at Barley Wood Walled Garden, thank you for the rhubarb leaves! Silki at The Forge for creating and sharing such a beautiful space. Feed Bristol, thank you for sharing your space. Flowers From The Plot, thank you for the beautiful flowers. The Cloth House, for the beautiful cloth and just generally existing. Wild Colours, for providing responsibly sourced dyestuffs. Matter Wholefoods, thanks for the onion skins! Chi Wholefoods, for the organic supplies. The Vintage Kitchen Store, Cornelissen & Son and Shepherds Bookbinders for all the beautiful things!

And for all my friends who I have not mentioned who have been there through this creative journey. I thank each and every one of my wonderful students who have attended my workshops, and their willingness to play and experiment with natural dyes. I learn so much from you and through sharing these beautiful techniques with you.

This book is offered in deep love of Earth and belief in the interconnectedness of all things. In dedication to bringing awareness to the way in which we make things, from soil to soil. May we find our way back to belonging and living harmoniously within our planetary home and local environments.

Managing Director Sarah Lavelle
Senior Commissioning Editor Harriet Butt
Assistant Editor Oreolu Grillo
Designer Katy Everett
Photographer Kim Lightbody
Head of Production Stephen Lang
Production Controller Martina Georgieva

Content taken from *Botanical Inks* (2018)
978 1 78713 156 9

Published in 2023 by Quadrille, an imprint of Hardie Grant Publishing

Quadrille
52–54 Southwark Street
London SE1 1UN
quadrille.com

Printed in China using soy inks